Contents

CW01546563

Introduction   2

EYFS Matching Chart   6

Festivals Matching Chart   8

The Entrance Area   10

The Home Corner   16

Books Everywhere   28

Outdoor Play   42

Maths Everywhere   54

Stories and Storytelling   68

Glossary   84

Brachot   92

Bibliography   100

Ben Zoma said, 'Who is wise? The one who learns from everyone'. (*Pirkei Avot* 4:1)

בֶּן זוֹמָא אוֹמֵר, אֵיזֶהוּ חָכָם, הַלּוֹמֵד מִכָּל אָדָם.

This book is a celebration of Jewish early years practice. It offers a host of new ideas and easily accessible practical activities to integrate the Jewish curriculum with the statutory Early Years Foundation Stage (EYFS 2008).

Young children have an inborn sense of wonder and are bubbling with uninhibited curiosity. Like Ben Zoma, they learn from everything and everyone. Their investigations of their surroundings lead them to draw personal and unique conclusions about the world around them.

It is an exciting responsibility to help children to extend their knowledge and to make connections between their different experiences. Blending Jewish learning with the EYFS can be both challenging and creative.

In this book, Jewish experiences follow four broad strands which flow through each chapter. These are:

- Thanks to God as Creator of the world.

- Caring for others and for the environment.

- Active participation in the ancient and ongoing Jewish story.

- Attachment to the land and people of Israel.

Why is this book different?

In Jewish early years classrooms, many hours are spent planning a programme that engages children in active discovery of their heritage. The ideas in this book build on the existing repertoire and open up new learning potential.

The focus is on using the whole environment to meet children's individual needs. Questions such as 'What *Pesach* activities can we provide for the children who learn best outdoors?' or, 'How can we involve Tali, who watches events from the security of the home corner?' replace, 'What activities can we do this year?'.

Outdoor options could include building an obstacle course to cross the Red Sea or mixing 'mortar' and moulding 'bricks' for Pharaoh. Indoors, make *Pesach* in the home corner for Tali (and others!) by adding a *Haggadah*, *matzot* and *Seder* plate or providing cloths, brushes and pans to clear the *chametz*.

Planning that is specific to one child will open up active learning opportunities for many.

Who is the book for?

- Everyone working in a Jewish early years setting.

- Staff in early years settings who want to include Jewish content in their planning.

- Anyone working to the EYFS.

How this book is structured

- Chapters focus on the learning environment: The Entrance Area, The Home Corner, Books Everywhere, Outdoor Play, Maths Everywhere.

- A chapter of original and traditional stories provides a starting point for introducing new concepts.

- Charts at the beginning give page references for festival activities and for EYFS links.

- A glossary (p. 84) gives transliterations with simple explanations of the Hebrew and Jewish terms used in the book. All italicised words in the text appear in the glossary.

- Blessings for a variety of occasions are referred to throughout, and can be found on p. 92–99 with transliteration and translation.

- The bibliography is arranged under sub-headings, such as festivals, Bible stories and Jewish life. It includes details of all the books referred to in the text, a range of Jewish books for young children and reference books for adults.

Chapters contain the following sections:

- **Introduction** – includes 'What matters to children?', 'Adult role', 'Reflection'.

- **Jewish values in action** – raises awareness of everyday 'Jewish moments'.

- **Experience Israel** – gives practical ideas to bring Israel into children's lives.

- **Jewish seasons and celebrations** – looks at each classroom area through the Jewish year (not included in The Entrance Area).

- **More ideas to explore** – highlights a Jewish perspective for a wide range of activities (not included in The Entrance Area).

- **Activities for immediate impact** – uses everyday resources to transform the environment whatever the time of year.

- **EYFS links** – references the chapter content to the EYFS.

Using this book – The Learning Environment

Use each chapter as a springboard to look at the potential for Jewish learning in every area of your setting. Usually, simple additions are all you need.

Candlesticks and a *Kiddush* cup in the home corner enable children to re-create their *Shabbat* experience in their play. A picture book of Noah and rainbow chalks added to a 'rainy day' weather box links the weather to biblical times and God's presence in the world.

With a little forward planning, the candlesticks and *Kiddush* cup can be part of a *Shabbat* box (see the activity on p. 24), and the weather box (p. 49) can include illustrated brachot for thunder and lightning and a rainbow (p. 92–93).

Festivals

To find ideas relating to festivals in each area, use the Festival Matching Chart on p. 8 where, for example, you will find *Succot* in the home corner on p. 21 and outdoor props on p. 46. Mathematical aspects of the festival are on p. 58 and a selection of books is given on p. 32. A new *Succot* story is included in the story chapter on p. 74.

Special and additional needs

While every child has individual learning needs, some children have specific difficulties, physical, sensory, emotional or cognitive. For others, English may be an additional language. Gifted children also have unique needs, to be considered in the context of the child's all-round development. Meeting the needs of every child is challenging; it is in response to this that ideas in this book are open-ended and non-prescriptive. Select what is right for the individual children in your setting and adapt to ensure that everyone has an opportunity to take part. For example, ensure that children with hearing or visual impairment can see the pictures and follow a story.

ICT

- Digital photographs used throughout illustrate how technology can be used as a learning tool for adults and children. Memory books (see p. 38) are an example of this in practice.

- For those with an interactive whiteboard, photographs taken in the setting can be displayed as a trigger for conversation about recent events and celebrations.

- Interactive games and programmes on Jewish topics, for children to use independently, are available on the Internet.

- Programmable toys can be used in a Jewish context, such as tracking across a map of Israel (see p. 51).

- Develop a listening corner by recording the stories in this book and adding headphones for children's independent use.

EYFS

The Early Years Foundation Stage (2008) is the statutory framework in England for learning, development and care of children from birth to five. It is centred on four themes which embody the following principles:

- A Unique Child (UC) – 'every child is a competent learner from birth who can be resilient, capable, confident and self-assured'.

- Positive Relationships (PR) – 'children learn to be strong and independent from a base of loving and secure relationships'.

- Enabling Environments (EE) – 'the environment plays a key role in supporting and extending children's development and learning'.

- Learning and Development (L&D) – 'children develop and learn in different ways and at different rates and all areas of Learning and Development are equally important and inter-connected'.

Each theme has a colour coded 'Principle into Practice' card. The quotations used in this book are taken from the cards and where page numbers are used, from the Practice Guidance for the Early Years Foundation Stage booklet (revised edition May 2008). The chart on p. 6 links the activities in the book to relevant EYFS statements.

Parallels for each of the themes can be found in Jewish texts:

- A 'unique child' is described in the *Talmud*, 'Just as there are no two faces exactly alike, so too there are no two people with exactly the same way of thinking'. (*Masechet Brachot* 5.9)

- 'Positive relationships' are fostered by 'loving your neighbour as yourself'. (*Vayikra* 19:18)

- A Jewish model of an 'enabling environment' is found in the *Shema* which recognises that learning takes place everywhere. 'You shall teach them (words of *Torah*) diligently to your children, talking of them when you are at home, when you go on your way, when you lie down and when you rise up,'. (*Devarim* 6: 6-7)

- 'Learning and development' go hand in hand when each child is 'educated according to his own way, and when he becomes old he will not depart from it'. (*Mishlei*: 22:6)

These texts provide an inspiring illustration of how the statutory and the Jewish curriculum can sit comfortably together, one reinforcing the other.

Chart for Principles into Practice Cards

This chart refers to the **Principles into Practice Cards** which illustrate how to apply the four themes of the EYFS.

It provides a quick reference to the pages where specific cards are quoted and highlights their practical application to the Jewish curriculum.

Cards / Chapters	A Unique Child	Positive Relationships	Enabling Environments	Learning and Development
The Entrance Area	1.3 p. 11 1.4 p. 14	2.1 p. 10, 11 2.2 p. 10, 11, 12 2.3 p. 14 2.4 p. 12	3.4 p. 10	4.3 p. 13
The Home Corner	1.1 p. 16, 17, 20 1.3 p. 18	2.1 p. 18 2.3 p. 26	3.1 p. 16, 24 3.2 p. 16, 22	4.1 p. 20 4.2 p. 24 4.3 p. 24 4.4 CLL p. 19 4.4 CLL p. 20 4.4 K&U p. 26
Books Everywhere	1.1 p. 34 1.3 p. 29	2.2 p. 28 2.3 p. 31	3.2 p. 30	4.1 p. 29 4.2 p. 38, 40 4.3 p. 38 4.4 p. 29 4.4 PSE p. 30 4.4 CLL p. 28, 30, 31,32, 34
Outdoor Play	1.1 p. 44, 46 1.4 p. 43	2.3 p. 46	3.2 p. 45 3.3 p. 42, 43, 46, 52	4.1 p. 49 4.3 p. 49 4.4 K&U p. 52 4.4 PSRN p. 50 4.4 PD p. 44, 45
Maths Everywhere	1.1 p. 66 1.4 p. 60	–	3.1 p. 55 3.2 p. 56	4.4 PSE p. 56 4.4 PSRN p. 54, 55, 57, 58, 60, 62, 64 4.4 K&U p. 55
Stories and Storytelling	1.1 p. 68	2.3 p. 68	–	4.2 p. 68 4.4 PSE p. 69

In addition there are six 'Learning and Development' cards, which relate to the six learning areas of the EYFS. These cards are numbered 4.4 in the book, and referenced in the 'Learning and Development column', with an abbreviated reference to the learning area:

PSE = Personal, Social and Emotional Development
PSRN = Problem Solving, Reasoning and Numeracy
PD = Physical Development

CLL = Communication, Language and Literacy
K&U = Knowledge and Understanding of the World
CD = Creative Development

Matching Chart to the EYFS Six Areas of Learning

This chart refers to the six areas of learning in the EYFS. It provides a quick reference to the pages where quotes from each area are used.

It highlights how all learning is interrelated and how closely the EYFS can blend with the Jewish curriculum. This chart is a starting point. There are many other links that can be found.

Areas / Chapters	Personal, Social and Emotional Development	Communication, Language and Literacy	Problem Solving, Reasoning and Numeracy	Knowledge and Understanding of the World	Physical Development	Creative Development	Introduction
The Entrance Area	p. 10, 11, 13, 14	p. 13	–	p. 13,14	p. 12	–	p. 12
The Home Corner	p. 16, 17, 18, 20, 22, 24, 26	p. 18, 22, 26	p. 24	–	–	–	–
Books Everywhere	p. 30	p. 28, 29, 30, 31, 32, 34, 40	p. 32	p. 38	–	–	–
Outdoor Play	p. 43, 45	p. 46	–	p. 43, 49, 50, 52	p. 42, 44, 45, 46, 50	p. 42, 49, 52	p. 42
Maths Everywhere	p. 62	p. 55	p. 54, 56, 57, 60, 64, 66	p. 54, 55, 60	p. 58, 62	p. 58	–
Stories and Storytelling	–	p. 68, 69	–	–	–	p. 69	–

All page numbers in the book refer to the Practice Guidance for the Early Years Foundation Stage (May 2008).

Festivals Matching Chart

Festivals Chart

This chart shows pages which feature ways of celebrating Shabbat and Festivals with young children and provides a quick seasonal reference for different areas of the classroom, indoors and out.

Chapters / Festivals	The Home Corner	Books Everywhere
Shabbat and *Havdalah*	p. 16, 17, 22, 24, 25	p. 35, 38
Rosh Hashanah	p. 20, 21	p. 32
Yom Kippur	p. 21	p. 32
Succot and *Simchat Torah*	p. 21	p. 29, 32
Chanukah	p. 21, 23	p. 32
Tu Bishvat	p. 21	p. 32
Purim	p. 21	p. 32, 40
Pesach	p. 21	p. 32, 33, 36
Yom Ha'ztmaut	p. 21	p. 33
Lag B'omer	–	–
Yom Yerushalayim	–	–
Shavout	p. 21	p. 33
17 Tammuz to 9 Av	–	–

The Entrance Area is not included as there are no references to specific festivals in that chapter.

Outdoor Play	Maths Everywhere	Stories and Storytelling	Chapters
			Festivals
p. 45, 52, 53	p. 54, 56, 60	p. 77	Shabbat and Havdalah
p. 46	p. 58	p. 70, 71	Rosh Hashanah
p. 46	–	p. 73, 74	Yom Kippur
p. 46	p. 58	p. 74, 79	Succot and Simchat Torah
p. 46	p. 56, 58	–	Chanukah
p. 47	p. 58	–	Tu Bishvat
p. 47	p. 58	–	Purim
p. 47	p. 56, 59, 64	–	Pesach
p. 47, 50	p. 57	p. 76, 80	Yom Ha'ztmaut
p. 48	–	–	Lag B'omer
p. 48	–	p. 82	Yom Yerushalayim
p. 48	p. 59	p. 72	Shavout
p. 48	–	–	17 Tammuz to 9 Av

Introduction

> Greet everyone cheerfully.
> (*Pirkei Avot* 1:15)
>
> וֶהֱוֵי מְקַבֵּל אֶת כָּל הָאָדָם בְּסֵבֶר פָּנִים יָפוֹת.

Start the day with a smile. By the time children arrive they may have been up for hours, dressed against the clock and left a half-eaten breakfast behind. A personal greeting makes a child feel recognised as an individual as s/he merges into the group. A warm welcome and a familiar routine help children to manage the transition between home and school.

You could make it part of your routine to introduce Hebrew words of welcome such as *Shalom* or *Boker Tov*. It is also a good time to mention special *Shabbat* and festival activities to parents. A personal word is much more effective than a note lost in transit.

- Plan for a staff member to greet families at the beginning and end of the session.
- Have Hebrew words of welcome on display.

What matters to children?

- Feeling secure.
- A familiar routine.
- Time to say goodbye.

Adult role

- Welcome everyone by name.
- Allow time for individual needs.
- Draw attention to current activities.

Reflection

- Does the entrance area feature in your planning?
- Do you have arrangements for providing private space if it is needed?
- Are all staff involved in welcoming families?

EYFS Links

Principles into practice cards

A welcoming atmosphere with approachable staff helps to create effective communication.
PR 2.2

Involve parents at transition times, valuing what they say and encouraging them to stay with their children while they settle in.
EE 3.4

Be aware that many factors will influence children's and families' sociability. They may be tired, stressed or trying to communicate in more than one language.
PR 2.1

Effective practice

Establish routines with predictable sequences and events.
(p. 33)

Planning and resourcing

Seek and exchange information with parents about young children's concerns so that they can be reassured if they feel uncertain.
(p. 30)

Jewish Values in Action

Respect – כָּבוֹד *Kavod*

R. Eliezer said, 'Let your friend's honour be as dear to you as your own'.
(*Pirkei Avot* 2:5)

רַבִּי אֱלִיעֶזֶר אוֹמֵר: יְהִי כְּבוֹד חֲבֵרְךָ חָבִיב עָלֶיךָ כְּשֶׁלָּךְ.

Care and mutual respect are the basis of successful relationships. Every school community – staff, children and their families – functions best with shared expectations. Staff and parents alike will respect the setting's standards if they know exactly what they are from the start.

In order to promote the Jewish philosophy, staff need opportunities to discuss it together, so that they become confident in sharing it with parents and handling any issues respectfully and sensitively.

Parents receive literature from the school, and there may be home visits, school visits and meetings. Usually the best communication is personal so give as much time as possible to direct meetings between staff and parents to establish trust and understanding.

In a way there are two 'entrance areas', the settling-in process and the physical space. The settling-in process is the start of the relationship between the family and the setting, a time for private and group interaction. Some parents need ongoing confidential time to discuss things that they are uncertain about, including aspects of Jewish practice.

- Make everyone who crosses the threshold feel comfortable and included by answering their questions, explaining what you are doing and listening to their contributions.

- Devote in service training to your Jewish philosophy so that all staff can discuss it respectfully with parents and families.

- Vary the timings of events and celebrations so that everyone has an opportunity to participate.

- Invite families to share their personal customs and traditions.

- Celebrate the diversity of Jewish communities from all over the world. Start with families in your group. Use Israel, with its vibrant population as a resource for multi-cultural education.

EYFS Links

Principles into practice cards

Having consistent boundaries for behaviour at home and in the setting helps children feel confident because they know what is and is not acceptable in either place.
UC 1.3

When each person is valued for who they are and differences are appreciated, everyone feels included and understood, whatever their personality, abilities, ethnic background or culture.
PR 2.1

Professional relationships with parents are based on friendliness towards parents, but not necessarily friendship with parents.
PR 2.1

All practitioners will benefit from professional development in diversity, equality and anti-discriminatory practice whatever the ethnic, cultural or social make-up of the setting.
PR 2.2

Effective practice

Share with parents the rationale of boundaries and expectations to maintain a joint approach.
(p. 35)

Jewish Values in Action
Creating Jewish Space

Principles into practice cards

Make sure that everyone who enters the setting receives a friendly welcome.
PR 2.2

Imagine what your setting seems like to a parent and their child when they first arrive.
PR 2.4

Effective practice

Take time to review individual needs for space and equipment for a child who may require modifications to either or both.
(p. 98)

Planning and resourcing

Regular information should be provided for parents about activities undertaken by the children; for example through wall displays, photographs and examples of children's work.
(p. 06)

> How goodly are your tents O Jacob.
> (*Bamidbar* 24:5)
>
> מַה טוֹבוּ אֹהָלֶיךָ יַעֲקֹב.

This blessing was given to the Children of Israel in the wilderness by the pagan prophet *Bil'am*. It is quoted in the prayer recited on entering a synagogue. The first step into a synagogue sets its character and atmosphere. In the same way, the entrance area to a nursery or school, which is the first thing that visitors see, makes a strong impression. Even though the space may be limited and the surroundings impersonal, you can create a welcoming atmosphere with simple bright furnishings. Recent festival photographs or a giant class-made *mezuzah* will draw attention to your setting as a Jewish space.

Whether it is purpose-built, a corridor or part of the classroom, the entrance area has to cope with a lot of traffic. Adapting it, to make space for adults or children with disabilities, parents with babies or even such down-to-earth skills as putting on your own coat, demonstrates your values in action.

- Try coming into your entrance area 'for the first time'. How does it make you feel?
- Create up-to-date displays which let parents know what's happening.
- Display copies of the latest notices or newsletters.
- Give parents their own bulletin board and/or suggestion box.
- Welcome visitors by including them on a 'what's happening today' board.
- Provide a box of board books or toys for parents waiting with babies.

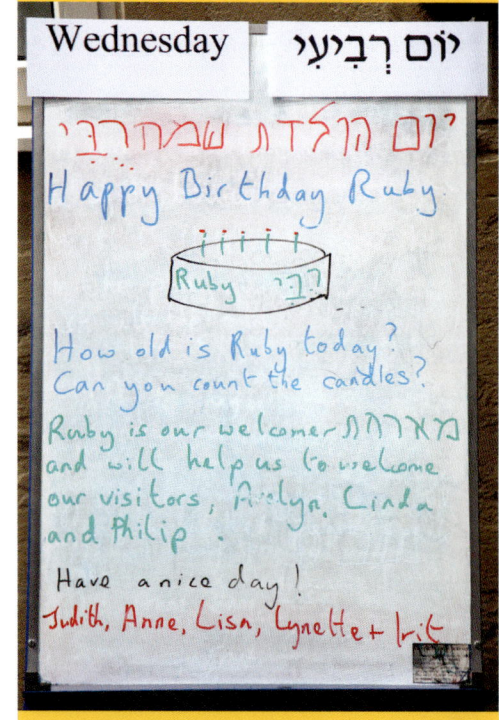

Experience Israel in The Entrance Area

My heart is in the East and I am at the far end of the West.
(Yehudah Halevi, 11th Century Poet)

לִבִּי בַמִּזְרָח וְאָנֹכִי בְּסוֹף מַעֲרָב.

After the destruction of the Second Temple in 70 CE, and the expulsion of the Jewish people from their land, longing for Israel was always at the heart of Jewish belief. The attachment remains as strong today and is an integral part of early Jewish education. For the youngest children, making a tangible link with Israel starts at the door, with Hebrew writing and images of Israel.

To give children a sense of belonging and instant recognition, use their photographs on their coat pegs and add their names in Hebrew and English. Display photographs of the people the children meet regularly at school or nursery.

If space allows:

- Put up a personalised map of Israel showing family and staff connections. You could attach labels to the places where relatives live, for example, Zoe's uncle in Beersheba.

- Display 'our Israel family' in photographs around the map.

- Create a welcome sign in English and Hebrew – *B'ruchim Haba'im*.

EYFS Links

Principles into practice cards

Document children's learning through photos and words. Use these to talk to children and parents about the learning that has taken place. **L&D 4.3**

Effective practice

Draw attention to marks, signs and symbols in the environment and talk about what they represent. Ensure this involves recognition of English and other relevant scripts. **(p. 59)**

Extend children's knowledge of cultures within and beyond the setting through books, videos, DVDs and photographs. **(p. 91)**

Planning and resourcing

Make a display with the children, showing all the people who make up the 'community' of the setting. **(p. 31)**

Activities for Immediate Impact
Talking About Children's Hebrew Names and Their Meanings

EYFS Links

Principles into practice cards

Children feel a sense of belonging in the setting when their parents are also involved in it.
UC 1.4

The more practitioners know about each child, the better they are able to support and extend each child's learning.
PR 2.3

Effective practice

Help children to learn each others' names, for example through songs and rhymes.
(p. 39)

Make the most of opportunities to value children's histories. Involve families in sharing memories.
(p. 86)

Planning and resourcing

Collect stories for, and make books about, children in the group.
(p. 26)

Children's Hebrew names, as in Leah's choice of name for her fourth son, have meaning and are traditionally a link with past generations. The name Yehudah became the name of the whole people – Jews are 'Yehudim'.

The speaking and listening activity that follows can take place in any part of the classroom. However, its outcomes, such as dual language name cards and a poster of the children's names in Hebrew, can be used and displayed in the entrance area.

Rationale

There is more than one way of using Hebrew for names. Just as Hebrew names can be written in English script, English names can be transliterated into Hebrew, as in the photograph on p. 13.

However, Jewish children also have a Hebrew name with its own special significance. Naomi means 'pleasant', David means 'beloved', Yehudah means 'thanks to God'. Knowing their own Hebrew name and its meaning adds uniquely to a child's Jewish identity.

You will need

- A dictionary of Hebrew names.
- Each child's Hebrew name (if a child doesn't have a Hebrew name, create a confidential moment and support the family in choosing a Hebrew name they like).
- A simple 'story' of why the name was chosen.
- A laminated card showing the child's Hebrew name and photograph.

Getting started

- Ask parents to tell their children why they chose their Hebrew name.
- You could ask for a short written explanation so that you can read it with the child.
- Choose a listening area.
- Work in a small group with a staff member.
- Go round the group helping children to show their name card and tell the 'story' of their name.
- Have paper and marker pens available at a nearby table so that children can draw or try copying their name if they want to. Scribe their comments.

Further ideas

- Hold the activity on a regular basis. Children will develop their skills and pride in their name as the year progresses.
- Make a poster of the children's Hebrew names.
- If the children use name cards to self-register, have their English name on one side and their Hebrew name on the other.
- Make a class book of the children's Hebrew names with their drawings and comments.

- Find out more about the names. There may be biblical associations, or associations with more modern heroes and heroines.
- Have *Alef-Bet* letter shapes, cut from textured fabric or sandpaper, for children to match to their Hebrew names.
- Create *Alef-Bet* cards, one letter per card, and a 'letter line' with pegs, for children to handle and play with. Can they find any of the letters in their name?
- Play rhythm or clapping games using the children's Hebrew names.
- Include staff Hebrew names in these activities.
- All these activities can be adapted for a family workshop where children learn about their family's names as well as their own.

Reflection

- Do the children talk about their Hebrew names?
- Do parents ever comment on the Hebrew names?
- What have you learned about Hebrew names through this activity?

Home links

- Talk about family names.
- Look at a family tree together.
- Look at photographs of past generations of the family and talk about the people in the photographs.

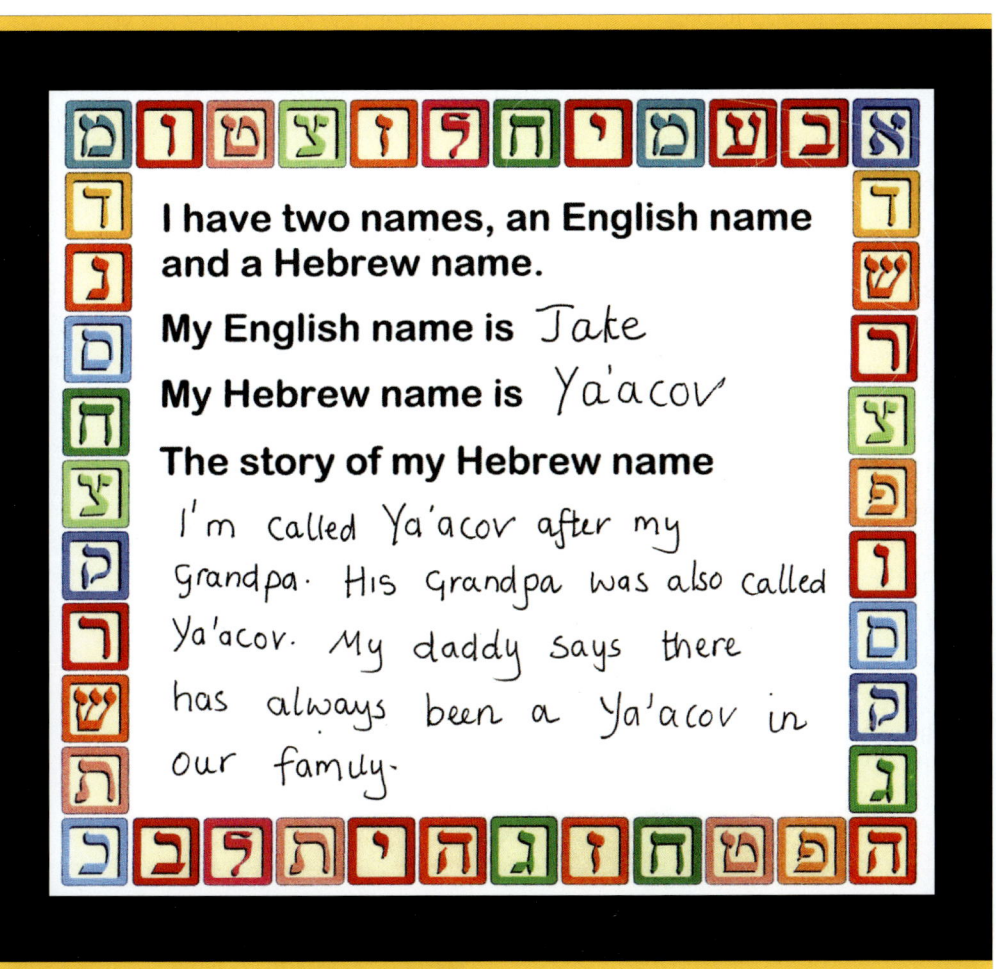

I have two names, an English name and a Hebrew name.

My English name is Jake

My Hebrew name is Ya'acov

The story of my Hebrew name

I'm called Ya'acov after my Grandpa. His Grandpa was also called Ya'acov. My daddy says there has always been a Ya'acov in our family.

Introduction

Let your house be wide open, let the poor be members of your household. (*Pirkei Avot* 1:5)

יְהִי בֵיתְךָ פָּתוּחַ לִרְוָחָה, וְיִהְיוּ עֲנִיִּים בְּנֵי בֵיתֶךָ.

The home is the place where family traditions evolve, as *Shabbat* and festivals are celebrated and life events build up a host of memories. Young children bring whatever they know to nursery or school, and this is reflected in their play, using the materials available. Simple additions to the home corner such as a *tzedakah box*, play money and *Shabbat* candlesticks provide a gentle introduction to Jewish life and values.

In a home corner full of Jewish things, children have their own space to relive their experiences through spontaneous play. Resources that change to reflect the Jewish year give them opportunities to reinforce what they have learned. Whether they are absorbed in solitary activities or interacting with others, children's play provides insight into their views of Jewish life, some of which may be surprising. Start from the child's Jewish perspective and plan activities to extend and deepen understanding all round.

Space is always at a premium but make the home corner as large as possible. Equip it with Jewish resources such as a *mezuzah*, a *Chanukiah*, a packet of *matzot,* and create a place buzzing with Jewish possibilities.

What matters to children?

- Unhurried time in the home corner to recreate experiences.
- The option to bring equipment from other areas to add to play.
- Resources that appeal to both boys and girls.
- Sensitive adults who listen, respond and inform without dominating.

Adult role

- Take a good look at your home corner. Is it a 'Jewish space'?
- Add varied resources to reflect the cycle of the Jewish year and events in children's lives, such as moving house or the birth of a sibling.
- Keep some festival resources available after the event so that children can revisit and recreate memories.
- Be flexible – children may make 'homes' in other areas inside and out.
- Display photographs of home corner activity, showing Jewish life and linked to the EYFS.

Reflection

- Does the home corner reflect the range of Jewish customs of the children in your group?
- What new knowledge are you gaining about the children's Jewish understanding?
- How are you adapting your planning to meet the children's needs?
- How effectively do adults share their insights?

EYFS Links

Principles into Practice cards

What children can do is the starting point for learning.
UC 1.1

Planning always follows the same pattern – observe, analyse and use what you have found out about the children in your group so that you can plan for the next steps in their learning.
EE 3.1

Use the experiences children bring from home, such as their family, the shops or the park, as starting points for their learning.
EE 3.2

Effective practice

Encourage children to talk about their own home and community life, and to find out about other children's experiences.
(p. 30)

Planning and resourcing

Provide a role-play area, resourced with materials reflecting children's family lives and communities.
(p. 33)

Provide activities and opportunities for children to share experiences and knowledge from different parts of their lives with each other.
(p. 40)

Jewish Values in Action
Hospitality – הַכְנָסַת אוֹרְחִים *Hachnasat Orchim*

And he (Abraham) said, 'My lords, if it please you, do not go past your servant. Let a little water be brought; bathe your feet and recline under the tree. And let me fetch a morsel of bread that you may refresh yourselves'.
(*Bereishit* 18:3,3–5)

וַיֹּאמַר אֲדֹנָי אִם-נָא מָצָאתִי חֵן בְּעֵינֶיךָ עַל-נָא תַעֲבֹר מֵעַל
עַבְדֶּךָ. יֻקַּח-נָא מְעַט-מַיִם וְרַחֲצוּ רַגְלֵיכֶם וְהִשָּׁעֲנוּ תַּחַת הָעֵץ.
וְאֶקְחָה פַת-לֶחֶם וְסַעֲדוּ לִבְּכֶם.

EYFS Links

Principles into practice cards

Support babies and children to develop a positive sense of their own identity and culture, this helps them to develop a positive self image.
UC 1.1

Effective practice

Children must be provided with experiences and support which help them to develop a positive sense of themselves and others; respect for others; social skills; and a positive disposition to learn.
(p. 24)

Abraham provided a warm welcome for strangers, starting a tradition of care which extends from family to the wider community. In biblical times, people welcomed guests by washing the dust of the desert off their feet as well as offering them food and drink. Today, it is a custom to invite strangers visiting a synagogue to share a *Shabbat* or festival meal with members of the community (see story 6, p. 75).

Nurseries and Reception classes are places where children can learn about Jewish aspects of hospitality, through adult example and planned activities. When you invite visitors to share *Shabbat* and festivals, involve the children from the start. Deciding who to invite, planning what food to eat, shopping and cooking are all activities which children find absorbing and tackle with enthusiasm. Greeting guests, on the other hand, may be a new and daunting experience. Young children are often shy but curious as well, and the more confident children will approach guests with questions. Over time, children will learn how to welcome and interact with visitors.

The home corner provides a natural environment in which to practise. With just a few extra items, children can invite guests, real or imaginary, to festival meals and birthday parties. Encourage them to find the things they need for their play, such as specific 'food', card for invitations and party clothes.

Encourage children to:

- Think up ideas for festival food, real and fantasy.

- Make shopping lists.

- Look out for kosher food and Hebrew writing on packaging.

- 'Bake' and 'cook'.

- Post/deliver invitations.

Jewish Values in Action
A Peaceful Home – שָׁלוֹם בַּיִת *Shalom Bayit*

> Hillel said, 'Be one of the disciples of Aaron, loving peace and seeking peace'.
> (*Pirkei Avot* 1:12)
>
> הִלֵּל אוֹמֵר: הֱוֵי מִתַּלְמִידָיו שֶׁל אַהֲרֹן, אוֹהֵב שָׁלוֹם וְרוֹדֵף שָׁלוֹם.

EYFS Links

Principles into practice cards

Explaining boundaries, rules and limits to children helps them to understand why rules exist.
UC 1.3

Help children who find it difficult to get on with others by showing them how to play and be friendly with other children.
PR 2.1

Effective practice

Show children how to use language for negotiating, by saying 'May I...?', 'Would it be all right...?', 'I think that...' and 'Will you?' in your interactions with them.
(p. 47)

Ensure that children have opportunities to join in. Help them to recognise and understand the rules for being together with others, such as waiting for a turn.
(p. 33)

Aaron, Moses' brother, was known for going out of his way to bring peace between people. The concept of *Shalom Bayit*, literally 'a peaceful home', is about how people live together in harmony, through mutual respect and positive interaction. This is a challenge for young children who often experience strong emotions which they find difficult to control. Children who frequently play with others learn how to share out different roles and equipment, take turns, listen to each other and communicate their needs. Conflict is inevitable, so teach negotiating skills.

- Model key phrases such as 'When can I have a go?'.
- Involve children in working out how to give everyone a turn.
- Work with children to produce a set of classroom rules. Keep it short, simple and use photographs to illustrate each rule.
- Notice little signs of caring, self-control and personal achievement. A smile, a nod or a quiet word does wonders for a child's self-esteem.

Create a *Shalom Bayit* board to provide a Jewish context to share children's growing social skills.

- Set up a board or wall space at child height. Make it eye-catching and include the words *Shalom Bayit*.
- Display photographs of children co-operating in play, or helping to give out drinks, and add the children's own words for captions.
- Use photographs to remind children of the class rules.
- Record special moments; you could use novelty post-its or speech bubbles.
- Add to and change the display regularly.
- Ensure that every child has at least one entry.

Experience Israel in the Home Corner

They will pray to You in the direction of their land which You gave to their fathers, of the city which You have chosen and of the House which I have built to Your Name.
(Kings 1, 8:48)

וְהִתְפַּלְלוּ אֵלֶיךָ דֶּרֶךְ אַרְצָם אֲשֶׁר נָתַתָּה לַאֲבוֹתָם הָעִיר אֲשֶׁר בָּחַרְתָּ
וְהַבַּיִת אֲשֶׁר בָּנִיתִי לִשְׁמֶךָ.

EYFS Links

Principles into practice cards

Develop children's awareness of languages and writing systems other than English and communication systems such as signing and Braille.
L&D 4.4 CLL

This prayer was recited by King Solomon at the dedication of the Temple and has led to the custom of Jews facing towards Jerusalem when praying. Wherever Jews live in the world, Jerusalem is their centre. The Hebrew word *Mizrach* means east, the direction of Jerusalem for Jews in the western Diaspora. It is also the name given to a decorative plaque, hung on the eastern wall of a home, to help people face the correct way when praying. Having a *Mizrach* in your home corner gives you an immediate link with Israel.

In addition to providing a *Mizrach*, make the most of other opportunities to bring Israel into the home corner, such as adding food packets with Hebrew writing, or an illustrated Israeli calendar.

Ideas to explore

- Use Hebrew words of welcome:

Shalom	Hello or goodbye (literally, peace)
Boker Tov	Good morning
Baruch Haba	Welcome (singular)
Bruchim Haba'im	Welcome (plural)

- Make a *Mizrach* for the home corner.

- Add books, newspapers, comics, magazines and greeting cards in Hebrew as well as English.

- Display posters with scenes from Israel and paintings by Israeli artists.

- When you label items, use Hebrew as well as English.

- Plan family events where parents and children can make a *Mizrach* or *Bruchim Haba'im* sign together. Think about the timing so that working parents can take part.

Jewish Seasons and Celebrations

> And you shall rejoice on your festivals and be very happy.
> (*Devarim* 16:14–15)
>
> וְשָׂמַחְתָּ בְּחַגֶּךָ וְהָיִיתָ אַךְ שָׂמֵחַ.

Many early years classrooms set up a festival interest area, with books, pictures and artefacts. This can be developed by making the items available on a Talk Table as an interactive activity during free play. Encourage children to examine and handle the objects with an adult on hand to listen to their ideas, talk about the items, add a personal reminiscence and share the books. Childproof versions of some of the artefacts, such as a metal *Seder* plate or a *Purim* shaker, can be placed in the home corner, to further enrich children's play (see story 3, p. 72).

Find your own balance between respectful use and everyday play. For example, how much of a plaything can a *shofar* be? When it is blown in a crowded synagogue, the *shofar* produces a raw sound that is intended to touch the hearts of the listeners, to make the 'Days of Awe' more awesome. A *shofar* that has been lying around in the home corner will not add meaning to anyone's experience of *Rosh Hashanah*. If it is sensitively introduced, however, children who have had a go at blowing it will anticipate the event with greater understanding. You will have to decide how much noise you can bear, but that's another issue!

Planning the transition between one festival and another is worth time and attention. It is a good idea to keep some resources in the home corner after a festival to trigger children's memories and add a Jewish element to their play. When it is time to put things away, children and staff can work together and decide on photographs for a class book and the festival frieze.

Festival resources

- White tablecloth, candlesticks, 'wine' bottle and wine cups.
- *Netilat Yadayim* cup.
- Homemade *Siddur* or *machzor* with basic *brachot*.
- Create a festival frieze at children's eye level. Display a photograph from your *Rosh Hashanah* celebrations, followed by one from *Succot*, then *Chanukah* and so on throughout the year. This will be a wonderful source for recall and conversation.

Ideas for Festival Role Play

Festival	Items to add to The Home Corner	Transform The Home Corner into
Rosh Hashanah *Yom Kippur*	• Apple and honey • Pomegranate • New Year cards • *Shofar* • Leather and non-leather shoes	Synagogue Post Office Clothes and hat shop Card shop Shoe shop
Succot	• *Lulav* and *etrog* • Pretend tools	*Succah* Carpenter's workshop
Chanukah	• *Chanukiot* and candles • *Dreidel* (*Sevivon*) • Latkes, doughnuts • *Chanukah* 'gelt' • Jugs/flasks	Doughnut/coffee stall Gift wrapping service
Tu Bishvat	• Fruit, plants • Pictures of trees of Israel	Garden centre Florist
Purim	• Dressing-up clothes • *Hamantaschen* • Food and baskets for *Mishlo'ach Manot*	Purim Palace Fancy dress shop *Mishloa'ch Manot* delivery service
Pesach	• Brush and pan • Cleaning cloth, bucket • *Haggadot* • *Matzah* and cover • Wine cups • Baby basket, Moses doll	Search for *Chametz* – provide torches, feathers and pan *Matzot* factory *Pesach* food shop Baby clinic
Yom Ha'atzmaut	• Israeli flag • Blue and white decorations • Food from Israel	Blue and white birthday party Travel agent El-Al plane Airport Falafel bar
Shavuot	• Flowers • Milky foods • Cheesecake • *Sifrei Torah*	Synagogue Ice cream and milkshake parlour Florist

More Ideas to Explore

EYFS Links

Principles into practice cards

Learning is a continuous journey through which children build on all the things they have already experienced and come across new and interesting challenges.
EE 3.2

Effective practice

Praise children's efforts to manage their personal needs and use and return resources appropriately.
(p. 38)

Establish opportunities for play and learning that acknowledge children's particular religious beliefs and cultural backgrounds.
(p. 25)

Planning and resourcing

Introduce children to books and other materials that provide information or instructions and carry out activities using instruction, such as reading a recipe to make a cake.
(p. 56)

Kashrut – Milk and Meat Dishes

Most home corners do not have the space for a milk and meat kitchen, but can fit in a vegetable rack to store two sets of colour-coded dishes for matching and sorting in a Jewish context.

Milk and meat storage areas can be labelled in Hebrew and English.
(see glossary, p. 84).

Recipe cards

The tastes of *Shabbat* and festivals are memorable and baking often features in early years activities.

- Use digital photographs to make a sequence of illustrated recipe cards for baking sessions.
- Make copies of the recipes to keep in the home corner. Children often 'cook' during role-play and recipes give them natural opportunities to link print and symbols with meaning.

Havdalah

Havdalah is the concluding prayer recited when *Shabbat* ends. It can be celebrated in the classroom on Monday or Tuesday.

- A plaited candle, wine and spices are used, and special blessings are said (see p. 96).
- If you celebrate *Havdalah* with the children, add a *Havdalah* set to the home corner for role-play.
- Grow sweet-smelling plants for *Havdalah* (see p. 52).

Washing feet

This is an unusual, fun activity that links a *Torah* story with a range of active-learning opportunities. Set the scene by telling the story of Abraham's visitors and why he washed their feet. Then recreate the activity and join in. Take your socks off, enjoy yourself and remember the *Torah* connection (see story 6, p. 75)!

- Provide towels, plastic bowls with a little warm water (bubbles optional), mopping cloths, chairs, separate containers for wet and dry towels, waterproof aprons.
- Work with a small group of foot washers and visitors. The 'visitors' sit down and are welcomed by the 'foot washers' who wash and dry their feet.
- Focus on self-help skills – taking off shoes and socks and putting them back on.
- Emphasise the importance of hygiene.
- Look at feet – wonder at the miracles of the human body.

How to make latkes

1. Peel

2. Grate

3. Mix

4. Fry

Activities for Immediate Impact
Provide a 'Shabbat Box' for Shabbat Play Every Day

And the Children of Israel shall keep the Sabbath, to make the Sabbath an eternal commitment (between God and Israel).
(*Shemot* 31:16–17)

וְשָׁמְרוּ בְנֵי־יִשְׂרָאֵל אֶת־הַשַּׁבָּת לַעֲשׂוֹת אֶת־הַשַּׁבָּת לְדֹרֹתָם בְּרִית עוֹלָם.

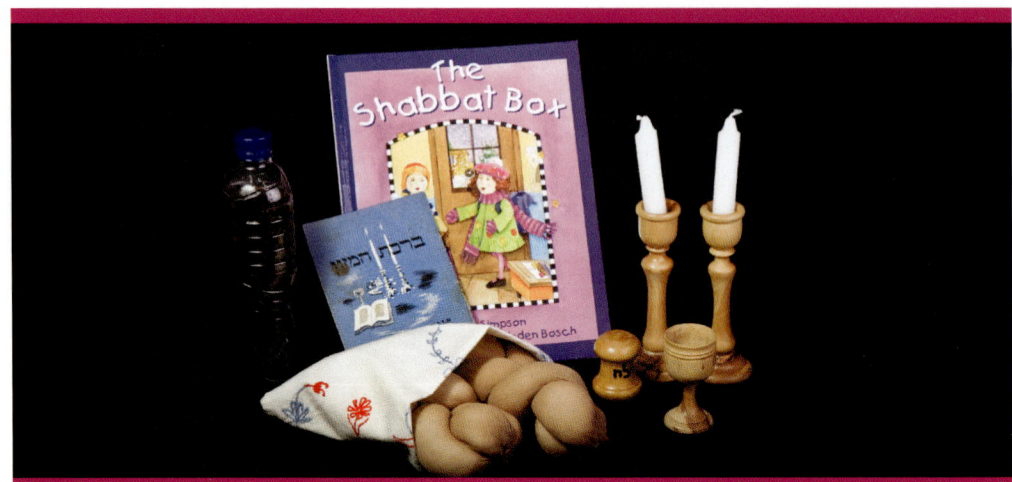

Rationale

A version of the 'Shabbat party' takes place in every Jewish nursery. Traditionally, children take turns to be 'abba' or 'imma' on a central *Shabbat* table, while the rest of the class sit around them in a circle joining in action songs. In a class of 25 children, each child has to wait weeks to be the *abba* or *imma*, recite the *brachot* and lead the activities. However, even when children have really looked forward to sitting at the *Shabbat* table they can find the experience overwhelming.

Give all the children opportunities to make *Shabbat* in their own time and space. Provide resources in a *Shabbat* box for them to use throughout the week during free play time. Let the children play. The adult role is to watch, learn and gain insight into each child's level of understanding.

You will need

- A decorated box, for example, shoe box to keep the *Shabbat* playthings in:

2 candlesticks and candles	Salt cellar
Brachot card or child's *Siddur*	Tablecloth
2 '*challot*' which can be made from plaited stuffed tights	*Kippot*
	Headscarves
'Wine' bottle	
Kiddush cups	
Challah cover	

- Checklist – stick a picture of the contents on the box lid so children can check that they have everything at tidy-up time.

- Story: *The Shabbat Box* by Lesley Simpson (see bibliography, p. 100).

Getting started

- Make your own 'Shabbat set', or buy a soft or wooden version.

- Decorate the box and fill it.

- Read the story *The Shabbat Box*, using your own box and contents as story props.

- Introduce the box to a few children at a time; encourage investigation and discussion.

- Make the box available during free play.

Further ideas

- Provide resources and/or activities that are reserved for Fridays. These 'Shabbat specials' could include shiny threading beads, glitter pens, *Shabbat* puzzles and games, fancy hats and dressing-up clothes.

- Start a new tradition. Have real flowers – just a few – for the *Shabbat* table or display area, contributed by different families each week.

- Prepare for *Shabbat* – provide cleaning cloths, a toy vacuum cleaner and brush and pan.

- Clean silver.

- Add tapes or CDs of *Shabbat* music to the listening corner.

- Cook for *Shabbat* in advance. Graduate from simple crackers or sandwiches to challot or cake as the year progresses. Encourage parents to contribute recipes and/or come and cook with the children.

- Create festival boxes. Add resources according to the time of year (see the chart on p. 21).

Reflection

- How do children use the *Shabbat* resources in their play?

- Do their ideas develop as the year progresses?

- How do staff and parents enrich the children's experiences?

- Does the *Shabbat* party fulfil its objectives? Could it be changed in any way?

Home links

- Lend the box to families over the weekend, on a rota basis. Include a notebook for parents to add their comments and their own *Shabbat* customs if they wish.

- Have a box of *Shabbat* books available for parents to browse through.

- Invite parents to contribute to a class book of traditional *Shabbat* and festival recipes.

Activities for Immediate Impact
Investigate *Mezuzot* with Children

You shall write them on the doorposts of your house and upon your gates.
(*Devarim* 6:9)

וּכְתַבְתָּם עַל־מְזֻזוֹת בֵּיתֶךָ וּבִשְׁעָרֶיךָ.

Rationale

A *mezuzah* on a doorpost is a sign of Jewish identity, and an acknowledgement of God's protection. These are both concepts children will absorb over time.

Mezuzot are usually placed too high for small children to see or touch. Give them opportunities to notice the *mezuzot* around them and to make 'their own' and fix them where they can reach.

You will need

- *Mezuzot* and cases.
- Magnifying glasses.
- Paper, felt-tipped pens, scissors and glue.
- Poster of Hebrew letters.
- Adhesive Velcro strips.
- Kitchen roll tube, box from toothpaste tube or similar for mezuzah cases.
- Box to store the children's play *mezuzot*.

Getting started

- Tell the *mezuzah* story (see p. 78).
- Show children a real *mezuzah* case and the scroll inside. Point out the letters representing the word 'Almighty' on the *mezuzah* case.
- Unroll the scroll and tell the children what it contains (the verses of the *Shema* that refer to the *mezuzah*).
- Have several *mezuzot* on a tray or table and magnifying glasses for children to investigate.
- Go on a *mezuzah* hunt.

Developing the activity

- Encourage children to 'write' their own 'scroll'.
- Provide paper (varied sizes) and materials as above.
- Put a poster of Hebrew letters at children's eye level.
- Accept all efforts.
- Provide boxes or tubes for '*mezuzah* cases,' decoration optional.
- See if children can insert the scroll into the case.
- Provide a place where children can put up their *mezuzot*, using Velcro. The entrance to the home corner is ideal.

Further ideas

- Keep the children's *mezuzot* accessible for them to use in play.
- Celebrate the arrival of your new children with a *mezuzah* fixing. Say the *bracha* with a few children at a time (see p. 98).
- Make a giant *mezuzah* for the entrance area.

Reflection

- Do children notice *mezuzot* around them?
- Are children developing pride in their own culture?

Home links

- Go on a *mezuzah* hunt on the way home, or at home.
- Invite parents to a '*mezuzah* evening'. The local rabbi could speak, a sofer (scribe) could demonstrate his skill and you could have a '*mezuzah* workshop' with cases for personal decoration.

Introduction

> And Esther's decree confirmed these matters of Purim and it was written in the book.
> (Esther 9:32)
>
> וּמַאֲמַר אֶסְתֵּר קִיַּם דִּבְרֵי הַפֻּרִים הָאֵלֶּה וְנִכְתָּב בַּסֵּפֶר.

Queen Esther's record of the customs of *Purim* is an early example of dramatic storytelling. When the *Megillah* is read today, children are drawn in by the excitement of listening for Haman's name.

That excitement is just one of a range of experiences that bring print to life long before children can decipher it for themselves.

Through sharing books with adults, children discover that they are treasure houses of information, fantasy and surprise. They gradually learn to 'read' the pictures, guess at meaning and make their own attempts at storytelling.

This chapter takes a fresh look at books from a Jewish perspective. There is a huge range of books for young children covering Jewish life, festivals and stories, including Hebrew versions of popular stories such as 'Where The Wild Things Are' and the 'Mr Men' series. Some settings have a 'Jewish book wish list', so that parents can choose to donate a book on their child's birthday.

Books belong in every area of the classroom, supported by a well-stocked book corner. A *Shabbat* book in the home corner, or 'Engineer Ari And The Rosh Hashanah Ride' by the train set may attract a child who doesn't often look at books.

- Select a few books and display them to excite the children's interest.
- Use your local library as a resource.
- Check that the book corner is warm, well lit and comfortable.
- Plan to have an adult available for storytelling during free play.
- Use puppets, soft toys and other story props.

What matters to children?

- Easy access to their favourite books.
- A caring adult to share a book with.
- Quiet time to enjoy a book or a picture.
- Space to sit or lie in comfort.
- Books featuring photographs of themselves.

Reflection

- When and how do children spontaneously use the book corner?
- When you plan, do you select books to support activities?
- How often do you review and renew your stock of books?
- Do you have a range of Jewish and Hebrew books?

Adult role

- Expect books to get worn through use – repairs to loved books are worth doing.
- Vary the books throughout the Jewish year.
- Respond to children's interests – find new books and pictures.
- Make books, using photographs of the children (see p. 38).
- Display photographs of the children reading.
- Use story props (see p. 40).
- Model reading and writing in different contexts.

EYFS Links

Principles into practice cards

Display lists of words from home languages used by children in the setting and invite parents and practitioners to contribute to them. Seeing their languages reflected in this way will encourage parents to feel involved and valued.
PR 2.2

Give daily opportunities to share and enjoy a wide range of fiction and non-fiction books, rhymes, music, songs, poetry and stories.
L&D 4.4 CLL

Planning and resourcing

Create an attractive book area where children and adults can enjoy books together.
(p. 56)

Ensure access to stories for all children by using a range of visual clues and story props.
(p. 56)

Jewish Values in Action
The Value of Knowledge

> Blessed are You, Lord our God, King of the Universe, Who has given of His knowledge to human beings.
> (Blessings on various occasions – *Siddur*)
>
> בָּרוּךְ אַתָּה ה' אֱלֹקֵינוּ מֶלֶךְ הָעוֹלָם, שֶׁנָּתַן מֵחָכְמָתוֹ לְבָשָׂר וָדָם.

This blessing, which is recited on seeing an outstanding secular scholar, illustrates the respect Jewish tradition gives to all learning. Every aspect of Jewish life can be enriched by general knowledge and stories. The prayer for rain on *Shemini Atzeret*, for example, can be a springboard for learning about the weather both here and in Israel. Children's activities and observations can be extended with Jewish stories such as Noah's Ark and Jonah and the big fish.

The chart below gives some ideas for Jewish books to enrich popular early years themes and areas of your classroom.

Homes	Light and dark
Hillel Builds A House	Good Morning Boker Tov
Shabbat Shalom	Goodnight Shema
Let's Build A Succah	It's Chanucah Time
My Jewish Home	Eight Candles To Light
A Mezuzah On The Door	Goodnight Lila Tov
A Sense of Shabbat	Shavua Tov
Myself	**Animals**
My Special Friend	All Afloat On Noah's Boat
Mitzvot I Can Do	The Littlest Frog
No Rules For Michael	Sammy Spider Series
The First Gift	Daniel And The Lions
Baby's Bris	
Rebecca's Journey Home	
A Holiday For Noah	

(See bibliography, p. 100 for a full book list.)

EYFS Links

Principles into practice cards

Reading stories and poems about everyday events is a good way of helping children to focus on who they can trust and how to keep safe.
UC 1.3

Although these (the six areas of learning and development) are presented as separate areas, it is important to remember that for children everything links and nothing is compartmentalised.
L&D 4.4

Tell and read stories and encourage children to act them out.
L&D 4.1

Effective practice

Encourage children to use the stories they hear in their play.
(p. 56)

Jewish Values in Action

Prayer – תְּפִלָּה Tefillah

> And you shall take to heart these words that I command you today, and teach them over and over again to your children.
> (*Devarim* 6:6–7)
>
> וְהָיוּ הַדְּבָרִים הָאֵלֶּה אֲשֶׁר אָנֹכִי מְצַוְּךָ הַיּוֹם עַל-לְבָבֶךָ. וְשִׁנַּנְתָּם לְבָנֶיךָ.

These words have been a linchpin of Jewish education from biblical times and are taken from the *Torah*, Judaism's most treasured book. They also form part of a key Jewish prayer, the *Shema* which is found in the *Siddur*.

Just as you can have a *Chumash* or *Tanach* beside you when you tell a biblical story, you can introduce children to a *Siddur* during *Tefillah*. There are several children's versions available (see bibliography, p. 100). Alternatively, a homemade one using photographs of the children will immediately excite their interest.

When you teach *Tefillah* to children, do so a little at a time and give them a simple explanation. You could introduce the *Shema* by saying something like: 'It is written in the *Torah*; Jewish people have been saying it from the time of Moses.'

Gradually build on your explanations and text as the year progresses. If you are using a homemade *Siddur*, add pages with the new text and pictures. Keep the *Siddur* accessible to the children so that they can look at it in their own time. Respond to their interest and comments – this is vital to fulfil the commandment 'teach over and over again.'

Make *Tefillah* child-friendly by varying your approach. You could introduce different tunes and add actions. Here is an example for the *Shema*:

בְּשִׁבְתְּךָ בְּבֵיתֶךָ	Be'shivtecha beveitecha When you sit at home – make a house shape with your hands.
וּבְלֶכְתְּךָ בַדֶּרֶךְ	Uvelechtecha vaderech When you are out on the road – drum feet on floor.
וּבְשָׁכְבְּךָ	Uveshoch'becha When you lie down – gesture going to sleep.
וּבְקוּמֶךָ	Uvekumecha When you get up – jump up and stretch arms.

EYFS Links

Principles into practice cards

Children need sensitive, knowledgeable adults who know how to engage their interests and how to offer support at different times.
EE 3.2

Link language with physical movement in action songs and rhymes.
L&D 4.4 CLL

Plan activities that promote emotional, moral, spiritual and social development together with intellectual development.
L&D 4.4 PSE

Effective practice

Value children's contributions and use them to inform and shape the direction of discussions.
(p. 48)

Planning and resourcing

Give children opportunities to be curious, enthusiastic, engaged and tranquil, so developing a sense of inner-self and peace.
(p. 40)

Experience Israel

Next Year in Jerusalem.
(*Haggadah*)

לְשָׁנָה הַבָּאָה בִּירוּשָׁלָיִם.

The *Passover Seder* service ends with the call – 'Next Year in Jerusalem'. For two thousand years the return to Jerusalem was a cherished dream, sustained through Jewish literature and prayer. Now that Israel can be a real part of children's lives it is even more important to remember the dream, which started with God's promise to Abraham, Isaac and Jacob and continues today.

Set the scene for your biblical storytelling by showing the children a *Tanach* and finding the page. Read a verse or two aloud, and continue with a child-friendly version. Some familiar Bible stories are included in the story chapter of this book.

Modern Israel has its share of inspiring stories for young children, and new ones are published frequently. A selection can be found in the bibliography (p. 100). Search the Internet for 'children's books on Israel', to find up-to-date information on the latest publications and suppliers.

Digital cameras make it relatively easy to make your own books, with photographs of children, families and staff on holiday in Israel or spending time with friends or relatives there. Homemade books featuring the children in the class will be treasured by all (see p. 38).

Introduce story props. You could use dolls or small-world play people as a biblical or Israeli family who feature in your stories. They could be kept in the book corner for children's spontaneous storytelling.

Recommended books about Israel

'My Cousin Tamar Lives In Israel'

'Let's Visit Israel'

'Come Let Us Be Joyful'

'Joshua's Dream'

'Jonathan And The Waves'

(See bibliography, p. 100 for details.)

Ideas to explore

• Start an ongoing 'resource bank' of photos of Israel. Collect postcards, calendars, personal photographs and commercial images. Check websites, exhibitions and art galleries.

• Use the resource bank to create a wall frieze or book.

• Visit libraries and borrow books on Israel.

• Collect Israeli recipes, try them out and photograph the process.

• Use all the media to bring Israel into the classroom. See one of the live webcams of the Western Wall.

• 'Hunt for Hebrew writing' – go on a 'Hebrew' walk around the setting to find Hebrew writing. You could extend this to the school, synagogue and local area if appropriate. Did the children find a *mezuzah* or a *mizrach*?

Jewish Seasons and Celebrations
Starting Points for Festival Books

EYFS Links

Principles into practice cards

Give daily opportunities to share and enjoy a wide range of fiction and non-fiction books, rhymes, music, songs, poetry and stories.
L&D, 4.4 CLL

Planning and resourcing

Encourage children to add to their firsthand experience of the world through the use of books, other texts and information and ICT.
(p. 57)

Include books containing photographs of the children that can be read by adults and that children can begin to read by themselves.
(p. 56)

Provide picture books, books with flaps or hidden words, books with accompanying CDs or tapes and story sacks.
(p. 58)

Display interesting books about number.
(p. 68)

And you shall rejoice on your festivals and be very happy.
(*Devarim* 16:14–15)

וְשָׂמַחְתָּ בְּחַגֶּךָ וְהָיִיתָ אַךְ שָׂמֵחַ.

This list gives a brief idea of the range of books available for young children. There are further ideas in the bibliography and new titles appear all the time. Publishers to look out for include Kar Ben and Frances Lincoln. You can also use an Internet search engine to find children's books on a particular festival or topic.

Rosh Hashanah and Yom Kippur	It's Shofar Time Sammy Spider's First Rosh Hashanah Engineer Ari And The Rosh Hashanah Ride Happy Birthday, World The Shofar Calls To Us The Hardest Word Apples And Pomegranates
Succot	It's Sukkah Time! Hillel Builds A House Sammy Spider's First Sukkot
Chanukah	Lots Of Latkes Harvest Of Light Sammy Spider's First Hanukkah Jodie's Hanukkah Dig It's Hanukkah Time Rainbow Candles Hanukkah Oh Hanukkah
Tu Bishvat	Sammy Spider's First Tu B'shevat It's Tu B'Shevat Grandpa And Me On Tu B'Shevat
Purim	Sammy Spider's First Purim It's Purim Time The Purim Surprise
Pesach	Sammy Spider's First Haggadah Sammy Spider's First Passover It's Seder Time Let's Ask Four Questions Where Is The Afikomen?

Pesach continued	Only Nine Chairs
	The Mouse In The Matzah Factory
Yom Ha'atzmaut	It's Israel's Birthday
	Sammy Spider's First Trip To Israel
	Let's Visit Israel
	My First Hebrew Word Book
	Harvest Of Light
	Come Let Us Be Joyful
	Joshua's Dream
	Israel
	Israel A To Z
Shavuot	Sammy Spider's First Shavuot
	Ten Good Rules
	No Rules For Michael

(Full details of all books can be found in the bibliography, p. 100.)

More Ideas to Explore

EYFS Links

Principles into practice cards

Language, thinking and learning are interlinked; they depend on and promote each other's development.
UC 1.1

Allow children to see adults reading and writing and encourage children to experiment with writing for themselves through making marks.
L&D 4.4 CLL

As children develop speaking and listening skills they build the foundations for literacy, for making sense of visual and verbal signs and ultimately for reading and writing.
L&D 4.4 CLL

Planning and resourcing

Set up a listening area where children can enjoy rhymes and stories.
(p. 45)

Set up displays that remind children of what they have experienced, using objects, artefacts, photographs and books.
(p. 50)

Jewish source books

A *Chumash* or a *Tanach* and a *Siddur* have a special place in every Jewish classroom or nursery. Children will learn that these books are treasured by the way in which adults handle them. It is traditional to show love for holy books by kissing them as you would a loved one. Keep them somewhere special, maybe in a *Kodesh* corner, and use them regularly for *Tefillah* and biblical storytelling.

Jewish books for life events

There are books for young children written from a Jewish perspective on difficult subjects such as death and bereavement, adoption, blended families and disability. Keep them as a resource to share with parents. If the occasion demands and parents agree, share an appropriate book with a child. Examples include:

> 'Rebecca's Journey Home' – adoption from abroad.

> 'Where Do People Go When They Die?' – different ways of explaining death to a child.

> 'My Special Friend' – Downs Syndrome.

> 'Grandma's Soup' – memory loss in old age.

> (See bibliography, p. 100 for a full book list.)

The book area

Create an attractive, cosy area where children and adults can enjoy books together. During free play sessions, plan for a member of staff or a parent to be in the book corner, ready to read the children's favourites.

Aim to have a good range of books – stories familiar and new, books about the world around us, and songs and rhymes. Include Bible stories, books about Israel and the festivals, and Hebrew versions of familiar stories.

Gradually build up a store of props, for example props for Noah's Ark could include pairs of animals and play-people stored in a box that can double as the ark.

Listening area

Set aside a quiet corner as a listening area. Provide CD players and headphones which children can use independently, and include books and CDs of Jewish songs and stories.

A Jewish connection

Books belong throughout the setting, and can add a Jewish connection to many areas, inside and out. Display them where children can see and use them freely. Have a waterproof box with a collection of books outdoors, and change the selection from time to time. Some starting points are listed below.

Sand play – 'Israel'.

Outdoors – 'Hillel Builds A House'.

Mark-making – 'Sofer, The Story Of A Torah Scroll'.

Home corner/water play – 'My Jewish Home' (board book/polyvinyl bath book).

Dressing up – 'It's Purim Time'.

(See bibliography, p. 100 for a full book list.)

Scrolls

The *Torah*, the *Purim Megillah* and *Mezuzot* are all hand written on parchment scrolls, and *Ketubot* are often handwritten. Invite a *sofer* to demonstrate his/her tools and skills, or ask a rabbi to show children a *Sefer Torah*, *Megillah* or *Mezuzah*. Follow up by giving children materials to make their own scrolls: paper, Hebrew letters, black mark-makers of all sorts. See if you can include a quill pen (also see story 9, p. 78).

Talk tables

Arrange a variety of books and items for thought and talk. Encourage children to examine and comment on what they find. Have an adult available to listen and stimulate discussion.

You could do this with:

- The contents of your festival boxes.
- A *havdalah* set and a range of different smelling resources – plants, herbs and spices.

Class *Haggadah*

Follow up a '*Pesach* talk table' by using the children's drawings to create an original class *Haggadah*. Provide picture books for reference, paper and drawing materials. Encourage children to draw whatever aspect of the festival interests them. Record their comments and read them aloud. Make sure there is a page for each child and assemble the '*Haggadah*' into a book. Keep it where children can look at it. They will be very proud to find their own page and 'read' their words 'in print'.

Festival recipe books

When children have had a cookery session, follow up by looking at recipe books together and talking about recipes they have used. Encourage the children to think about how their favourite foods are made and 'write' or scribe their imagined ingredients and recipe method. Each child can decorate their own recipe page. Staple the children's personal recipes into a book as part of the festival celebration.

Cards for all occasions

- Greeting cards are not books, but they do enable young children to send messages by making marks on paper. Take time to listen and talk to them about their drawing or writing.

- Provide resources for card making. Include old greeting cards, card of different sizes, writing materials, glitter, scissors, shiny paper, glue and envelopes for children to use for *Rosh Hashanah*, *Chanukah*, birthdays etc. The more opportunities children have to experiment, the more confident and skilful they will become.

- Make a letterbox (you could use a painted shoe box) so that children can post their letters if they want to.

David's Pesach Pancake

You need sugar and put it in the mixer and it goes around and around. And then you add some milk. Oops it doesn't need milk. If you use milk, the pancake will burn. Put it on the stove; it has to be burned a little. Eat it with a fork.

Songs and rhymes

Jewish learning has always recognised that chanting is a powerful tool for teaching and memorising. Through tune, rhythm, rhyme and repetition, children absorb words and concepts that will stay with them throughout life. This is at the core of early years education.

Rhymes, rhyming stories and songs lift the atmosphere and draw children in. Children are uncritical and will respond even if you can't sing! Children who appear detached often go home word perfect.

Many of the books referred to in this chapter appeal to children through rhyme and repetition. Jewish songs and music for young children are available on CDs; some are listed below and new ones are issued frequently.

Example CDs

'Shirim al Galgalim' – Songs on Wheels by Debbie Friedman.

'Shiron L'gan' – Jewish songs for children ages 2–5.

'Shirei Chagim' – Songs for festivals, ACUM/Steimatzky CD series.

Activities for Immediate Impact
Make Jewish Memory Books Using Photographs of the Children

EYFS Links

Principles into practice cards

Document children's learning through photos and words. Use these to talk to children and parents about the learning that has taken place.
L&D 4.3

Look at children's involvement in their learning as well as the nature and quality of adult interactions in children's learning.
L&D 4.2

Effective practice

Make books of events in settings, for example, summer fair, building a climbing frame, shopping expedition or learning about a festival.
(p. 86)

Remember the days of old.
(*Devarim* 32:7)

זְכֹר יְמוֹת עוֹלָם.

Rationale

Jewish memory books are a way of remembering occasions the children have shared. They contain photographs which record an event such as buying and using a new *havdalah* candle or celebrating a teacher's wedding. Books use children's natural interest in photographs of themselves as a springboard for creative learning, based on first-hand experiences.

You will need

- A set of photographs which show the stages involved in preparing for and celebrating an event.

- Materials to make a loose-leaf book – for example, mounting card, glue, hole punch, string, pens.

- Written permission from parents or guardians to take photographs of the children.

- New books throughout each year, so that they feature children currently in the class.

Getting started

- Set up a 'photo table' where children can examine and talk about the photographs with an adult.

- Spend time with the children selecting the pictures you will use for the book.

- Mount each picture and use the children's words to add a caption.

- Ask children to help put the pictures in order and thread them together.

- Look at the book together.

- At circle time, introduce the book to the whole class. Children will want to 'read' their page to their friends.

- Keep all the books where children can look at them and read them to each other.

- Using *havdalah* as an example, a memory book could include photographs of:

  Buying a *havdalah* candle.

  Taking it out of the box.

  Children looking at it.

  Putting it in a holder.

  Assembling the things needed for the ceremony.

  Celebrating *havdalah.*

Further ideas

- Children can take their own photographs.
- Have a second set of photographs for sequencing.
- Make books using children's drawings.
- Personalise class-made *Siddurim* or *haggadot* with a child's own photograph.
- Use the children's own words in a speech bubble to caption displays and interest tables.
- Use the photographs in a wall frieze at children's eye level.
- Make a festival frieze (see p. 20).

Reflection

- Are all children represented in the class books over a period of time?
- Can children describe what is going on in a picture?
- Are they beginning to understand 'what came first' and 'what happened next'?
- How frequently do children choose to look at and talk about the memory books?

Home links

- Share the books with parents and carers.
- Use photographs in newsletters and parents' notice boards.
- Hold an occasional 'family photos' day when children bring in a favourite family photograph.

Sam's uncle Yossi works in this street in Jerusalem

Tali spotted 2 Magen Davids

Activities for Immediate Impact
Develop a Resource Bank of Props for Jewish Storytelling

EYFS Links

Principles into practice cards

Children benefit from a range of experiences, including those that are predictable, comforting and challenging.
EE 3.2

Active learners need to have some independence and control over their learning to keep their interest and to develop their creativity.
L&D 4.2

Planning and resourcing

Introduce alongside books, story props, such as pictures, puppets and objects, to encourage children to retell stories and to think about how the characters feel.
(p. 46)

In every generation people should see themselves as though they had personally come out of Egypt.
(*Haggadah*)

בְּכָל דּוֹר וָדוֹר חַיָּב אָדָם לִרְאוֹת אֶת עַצְמוֹ כְּאִלוּ הוּא יָצָא מִמִּצְרָיִם.

Rationale

This quotation highlights the essential quality of good storytelling – making the story live. Traditional Jewish stories can seem complex and removed from the children's lives, so it is a challenge to find ways for children to get 'hands-on' experience. Props make stories visible. Devising props helps adults to focus on the key elements of a story and enhance storytelling. When children use familiar props, they can rediscover the characters and action, talk about them and create their own versions.

You will need

- *Tanach* or *Megillah*.
- A child's version of the story.
- Props for the story.

For example, for *Purim* you could use:

Story line	Prop
Esther becomes queen	Crown or princess doll
Haman casts lots	Box and bits of card, or calendar pages
The chronicles are read to the King	Book with picture of king, or *Purim* story
Haman leads Mordechai around town on horse	Hobby horse or toy horse
Letter sent to communities in Persian Empire	Scroll
Mishlo'ach Manot	Basket with 'food' items

Getting started

- Tell the story using props. If you are new to this way of storytelling, start with one or two props only.
- Set up a talk table with the props, the story and the source book.
- Put the story and props in the book corner for children to use, with occasional adult input.

Further ideas

- Prop boxes – keep some stories and props in a box accessible to the children.
- Story line – make picture cards illustrating a recent story, for children to play with and talk about. Add a washing line and pegs for them to sequence the pictures and recreate the story.
- Story hide and seek – hide a book and set of props outside for the children to find and play with.
- Have a hat for each character of your story. This may well be all that children need to embark on a story adventure.

Reflection

- How have the props helped the adults in their storytelling?
- How have the props helped children to engage with Jewish stories?
- To what extent have props become an ongoing resource for telling Jewish stories?

Home links

- Let parents know which Jewish stories you are telling.
- Have a 'props needed' corner in your newsletter.
- Welcome parents who have time to share a story with the children.

Introduction

The heavens declare the glory of God, the sky proclaims His handiwork. (*Tehillim* 19)

הַשָּׁמַיִם מְסַפְּרִים כְּבוֹד-קֵל וּמַעֲשֵׂה יָדָיו מַגִּיד הָרָקִיעַ.

Biblical imagery often takes us out of doors. God promised Abraham that his seed would be like the stars of the heaven and Jacob that his descendants would be like the dust of the earth. Bible stories are usually told indoors but most take place outdoors. They often feature the natural world, the weather and families on the move.

The 'pilgrim festivals' of the Jewish year are shaped by the agricultural cycle. *Succot* is the 'Festival of Ingathering', *Pesach* is the 'Festival of Springtime', *Shavuot* is the grain harvest and the festival of the 'first fruits'. *Sefirat Ha'omer*, the Counting of the *Omer,* and *Tu Bishvat*, the New Year for Trees, celebrate the produce of the earth.

Rediscover the outside as a source of Jewish learning. Involve the children as you plan for outdoor events; dance with the *Torah* or cross the Red Sea. Maximise the time available for outdoor play. Pull on your wellies, experience the flood and paint a rainbow!

What matters to children?

- Freedom to move and explore.
- Opportunities to be noisy.
- Flexible provision of resources.

Reflection

- What percentage of their time do children spend outdoors?
- To what extent does the outdoors reflect the Jewish year?
- What have you learned through watching outdoor play?

Adult role

- Be prepared to go outside throughout the year.
- Create opportunities for Jewish learning outdoors.
- Use fixed equipment creatively, for example, use a blanket to transform the climbing frame into a *Succah* or Abraham's tent.
- Engage in children's play.

EYFS Links

Principles into practice cards

Being outdoors offers opportunities for doing things in different ways and on different scales than when indoors.
EE 3.3

Where possible link the indoor and outdoor environments so that children can move freely between them.
EE 3.3

Effective practice

Providing well-planned experiences based on children's spontaneous play, both indoors and outdoors, is an important way in which practitioners support young children to learn with enjoyment and challenge.
(p. 07)

Make time and space for children to express their curiosity and explore the environment using all their senses.
(p. 110)

Planning and resourcing

Provide time and space to enjoy energetic play daily.
(p. 97)

Jewish Values in Action
Caring for the Environment – בַּל תַּשְׁחִית *Bal Tashchit*

> And the Lord God placed man in the Garden of Eden to work in it and look after it.
> (*Bereishit* 2:15)
>
> וַיִּקַּח ה' אֱלֹקִים אֶת-הָאָדָם וַיַּנִּחֵהוּ בְגַן-עֵדֶן לְעָבְדָהּ וּלְשָׁמְרָהּ.

Use the story of Creation as a starting point for involving children in caring for the environment. Children who see the world as God's gift will want to look after it. Jobs which adults see as tedious are often great fun for children!

Young children have a natural appreciation of the wonders of creation. Being small they are close to the ground and see living things close up – a spider's web, a creepy crawly, a dewdrop, twigs and stones. Crouch down so that you can see things from the children's perspective. Be guided by their interest and allow time to look, talk and discover.

Put together a discovery box that includes magnifiers, bug viewers, binoculars, torches, tape measures, mirrors, photos of birds, insects, paper and crayons. To add a Jewish dimension, include blessings to say when you see a rainbow or lightning (see *Brachot*, p. 92), smell fragrant woods or bark, hear thunder or see fruit blossom for the first time. Help children understand the process of growth by growing *Pesach* festival foods such as lettuce and herbs. If you plant around *Tu Bishvat* you may have vegetables ready for the *Seder*.

Encourage children to:

- Sweep leaves.
- Collect litter.
- Be kind to animals, for example, feed the birds (*Tza'ar Ba'alei Chaim*).
- Compost biodegradable materials, for example, lunchtime leftovers.

EYFS Links

Principles into practice cards

Children gain a sense of wellbeing when they are encouraged to take responsibility and join in by helping with manageable tasks that interest them.
UC 1.4

Think about the food that your setting encourages children to enjoy. How do you help children learn about the food chain and planting, growing, gathering, preparing and using different foods?
UC 1.4

The outdoor environment gives children firsthand contact with the weather, seasons and the natural world.
EE 3.3

Effective practice

Demonstrate concern and respect for others, living things and the environment.
(p. 36)

Encourage young children to explore puddles, trees and surfaces such as grass, concrete or pebbles.
(p. 87)

Jewish Values in Action
The Miracle of the Human Body

> God created human beings… He created male and female.
> (*Bereishit* 1:27)
>
> וַיִּבְרָא אֱלֹקִים אֶת-הָאָדָם .... זָכָר וּנְקֵבָה בָּרָא אוֹתָם.

The miracle of the human body is most evident at birth and in the rapid growth of early childhood; for the very young, it is a source of wonder and discovery.

Babies are fascinated by their hands, toddlers work to balance on two feet, and older children are constantly testing what their bodies can and cannot do. They take pride in their achievements, whether it is grasping a toy, taking a first step or balancing on a wall. This spontaneous motor development takes place wherever the child may be. Planned activities outside add the extra dimensions of space, fresh air and the challenge of vigorous movement.

Children of all ages benefit from being outdoors, and for some it is the environment in which they learn best. Use children's natural exuberance and energy to explore Jewish experiences.

- Jump up to touch the *mezuzah*, or move like different animals into the 'ark'.

- Provide for large-scale construction alongside photos of Israeli landmarks.

- Celebrate festivals with song, dance and music-making without the constraints of walls.

- Make obstacle courses and encourage children to cross the 'desert' or the 'Red Sea'.

- Plan to include children with additional needs, for example put a *mezuzah* where a child in a wheelchair can stretch up to reach it.

Experience Israel Outdoors

> And I will give rain in your land in its season, the early and late rains,
> and you will gather in your corn, your wine and your oil.
> (*Devarim* 11:14)
>
> וְנָתַתִּי מְטַר-אַרְצְכֶם בְּעִתּוֹ יוֹרֶה וּמַלְקוֹשׁ וְאָסַפְתָּ דְגָנֶךָ וְתִירשְׁךָ וְיִצְהָרֶךָ.

Living in Israel has always been dependent on God's gift of rain. This can be a difficult concept for young children who live in a country where 'rain stops play'.

Much of Israel is waterless desert and yet today agriculture flourishes and its products are exported all over the world. Developing a nursery garden introduces children to caring for plants and watering them, which is even more essential in a dry country such as Israel. Children love playing with water and if you provide funnels, pipes and tubing they will experiment with transporting it from one place to another, as Israel does with its 'National Water Carrier'. You can find out more, including exciting pictures of pipes big enough for a man to climb into, by checking the Israel National Water Carrier on the Internet (see story 7, p. 76).

Use the Internet to find other images of Israel and familiarise children with the look of the country and its diverse population.

Ideas to explore

- Grow plants that also grow in Israel, such as cyclamen and rosemary.

- Create a biblical garden area with pots and tubs. Try growing as many of the 'seven species' (*Shivat Haminim*) as is practical. These are the plants listed in the *Torah* as characteristic of Israel. They are: wheat, barley, grapes, figs, pomegranates, olives and dates.

- Grow sweet-smelling plants for *Havdalah* (see p. 52).

- Start a tradition where parents donate a plant or seeds on their child's birthday.

- Become archaeologists – bury 'artefacts' for the children to find in the earth or the sand: stones with Hebrew letters on them, bits of 'parchment' or 'pottery', pieces of fabric, *kiddush* cups, Hebrew letters.

   Tell children the story 'Water in Israel' (see p. 76) and recreate giant pipes or Hezekiah's tunnel with pop-up and solid play tunnels and barrels.

- Create laminated photo cards of Israeli buildings, pipelines, sprinklers and scenery to inspire construction and imaginative play. Enlarge old calendar photographs or print images from the Internet.

- Paint or draw arches and domes on a range of boxes for 'Israeli style' large-scale construction.

EYFS Links

Principles into practice cards

Learning is a continuous journey through which children build on all the things they have already experienced and come across new and interesting challenges.
EE 3.2

Babies and children learn by being active and physical development takes place across all areas of learning and development.
L&D 4.4 PD

Effective practice

Establish opportunities for play and learning that acknowledge children's particular religious beliefs and cultural backgrounds.
(p. 25)

Planning and resourcing

Provide large portable equipment that children can move about safely and co-operatively to create their own structures.
(p. 98)

Jewish Seasons and Celebrations
Festivals Out of Doors

> And you shall rejoice on your festivals and be very happy.
> (*Devarim* 16:14–15)
>
> וְשָׂמַחְתָּ בְּחַגֶּךָ וְהָיִיתָ אַךְ שָׂמֵחַ.

Rosh Hashanah

- If you have access to an apple tree, collect windfalls and measure and record the children's height in apples. Use the apples afterwards to make apple cake or apple and honey compote.

- Have a 'honey' picnic, teddy bears optional.

- White is a traditional colour for *Rosh Hashanah* and *Yom Kippur*. Provide children with large sheets of coloured paper, big brushes, spreaders, rollers, sponges, white paint and let them experiment. The paper could be spread on the ground or on a wall.

Yom Kippur

- Add Jonah, a boat and a big fish to your water play.

- Turn the climbing frame or a large box into a whale!

Succot, Shemini Atzeret and Simchat Torah

- Provide materials and tools for *succah* building – blankets, string, garden chairs, a play-tent frame.

- Go on a real *succah* crawl, or devise your own route around the play area with a series of stops for refreshments.

- Introduce woodwork using soft wood offcuts.

- Provide resources for a *lulav* and *etrog* procession. Children can make their own *lulavim* and follow a route round the playground. Sing as you go!

- Encourage children to smell the *etrog* and find scented plants to talk about.

- For *Simchat Torah*, provide homemade or 'soft toy' *Sifrei Torah* to dance and sing with. Children can also use flags they have made.

- The phrase *Mashiv haru'ach umorid hageshem* ('Who causes the wind to blow and the rain to fall'), is added to the *Amidah* from *Shemini Atzeret* to the first day of *Pesach*. In the unlikely event that it doesn't rain, make your own! Provide watering cans and umbrellas. This is a good time to practise putting on wet-weather clothing.

Chanukah

- Make a giant *Chanukiah* from boxes or construction materials.

- Set up a working *Chanukiah* outside if possible.

- Spin *sevivonim* (*dreidels*), hoops and natural materials. What else spins?

- What happens to your body when you spin? How long does it take to return to normal? Devise ways to include any children with mobility difficulties.

- Set up a *latke* or doughnut stall.

Tu Bishvat

- Plant a tree in a garden or local park, or plant some seeds.

- Go on a 'tree discovery' walk. Take photos of different trees in the locality for children to find.

- Collect natural materials for outdoor collage. Provide 'connectors': string, ribbon, tape and glue.

- Hide 15 fruits for *Tu Bishvat* for children to find, then enjoy washing and eating them.

- Visit a garden centre and then set up an imaginative play one.

- Scramble over logs, climb trees; go to a natural play park if there is one locally.

- Look at logs to find tree 'rings' that show the age of the tree.

Purim

- Create a palace for children to discover, or provide the materials for them to make their own.

- Recreate Mordechai's 'procession' through the streets of Shushan. Make hobby horses, provide headdresses and cloaks. Draw a route with chalk, or children can plan their own route.

- Deliver *Mishlo'ach Manot* to neighbours or members of staff.

Pesach

- Wash large equipment outside. Provide soapy water and plenty of cloths.

- Provide imaginative play resources for 'digging like slaves'.

- Add red food colouring to the water tray. Provide plastic frogs and animals to link with the plagues.

- Use the water tray for 'crossing the Red Sea'. Provide large stones or pebbles for children to make a 'dry path', and plastic people and animals to cross over the path.

- Recreate the crossing with an obstacle course in the playground. Can children get across without touching the ground and 'getting their feet wet'?

- Build a '*matzah* oven' with large bricks and provide the tools – long-handled baking trays, aprons and hats.

- Mix 'mortar' in your sand or builder's tray. Use sand, water and earth and provide brick moulds.

Yom Ha'atzmaut

- Blow up blue and white balloons, then let them deflate and fizzle around – learn about the power of air.

- Dance with blue and white streamers.

- Weave blue and white ribbons or paper around poles or fences.

- Put out blue and white playground chalks.

- Hold an Israeli-style picnic with pitta, falafel, hummous, salad. Invite parents to join the celebration.

- Add Israeli flags to the outdoor construction resources.

Jewish Seasons and Celebrations
Festivals Out of Doors

Lag B'omer

- Do bonfire painting on a grand scale using big sheets of paper, fiery colours, brushes, rollers, sponges and glitter.

- *Lag B'omer* is a traditional time for weddings. Put up a *chuppah*, take dressing-up clothes and a *Kiddush* cup outside. Don't forget the camera!

Yom Yerushalayim

- Prepare two sets of laminated photographs of Jerusalem landmarks. Hide a set for the children to find and match.

- Enlarge photos of the landmarks, mount them on card and make floor puzzles.

Shavuot

- Tell the story of the giving of the *Torah* outside.

- Provide props for Mount Sinai in the sand tray – '10 commandments', flowers, play people.

- Discuss the 'outdoor safety' rules with the children, and display them outside.

- Tell the Story of Ruth (see story 3, p. 72).

- Set up a 'harvesting' role-play area with a selection of baskets and a heap of 'gleanings' (for example, straw, shredded paper, cardboard packing materials) for children to collect.

- Grow wheat from seed. It sprouts quickly indoors and can be taken outside. Use wheat seeds from a health food store.

- Set up an ice cream stall for dairy foods role-play.

- Plant seeds with the children early in the year to flower at *Shavuot*, or care for bedding plants.

- Set up a flower stall. If possible, visit one first.

17 Tammuz to 9 Av – The 'Three Weeks'

- Build a *Kotel* where the children can attach their 'letters to God' (see story 12, p. 82).

- Visit the local fire station and follow up with role-play.

More Ideas to Explore

Weather boxes

Create resource boxes with a Jewish perspective.

In all boxes include: paper, clipboards and drawing materials. Illustrate and laminate *Brachot* (see p. 92) and protect books in a plastic pouch. Take out the camera to record activities.

For specific weather conditions add:

- Rain: fabrics (waterproof and non-waterproof), transparent containers, umbrellas, waterproof hats, chalk to draw around puddles, small floating toys, the text *mashiv haru'ach umorid hageshem*.

- Thunder and lightning and rainbows *brachot* (see *Brachot,* p. 92).

- Wind: streamers, windmills, wind tunnel, bubbles, scarves (chiffon and woolly), flags, bells and wind chimes. Stories: 'Jonah' or 'Crossing The Red Sea'.

- Sun: hats, sunglasses, sun cream, parasols. Stories: 'Jonah' or 'Abraham And The Visitors'.

- Snow: magnifying glass, pictures of snowmen, gloves and woolly hats, scoops and containers. Stories: 'The Shabbat Box' or 'Lots Of Latkes'.

Make a well

Wells feature in many biblical stories. You can make one with a pulley and bucket attached to an 'A' frame or climbing frame. Children can experiment with moving a full bucket up and down. Challenge them to carry a jug balanced on their head. Have a go yourself!

Dens

A den is a secret place which children create for themselves. It can be as simple as a cardboard box or large blanket to huddle under. It is a space for children where they can be free from adult expectations. Making a den may be an end in itself or it may be the starting point for role-play.

Jewish people, traditionally wanderers, have often had to scrape together a home from whatever materials are available. Children do this instinctively, developing negotiation skills, imagination, spatial awareness, problem solving skills and a range of physical skills. Children who are familiar with Jewish stories and resources are likely to include them in their den making and imaginative play. The story 'Hillel Builds A House' is a good starting point.

- Possible resources for den making include: carpet squares, large pieces of fabric, boxes and crates, string, tape, pegs and *mezuzot*.

- Props for role-play include: sleeping bags, blankets, tools, suitcases and backpacks and candlesticks.

Themed backpacks

Backpacks make wonderful resource banks. They are easily stored and transportable. Keep them on hooks accessible to the children, for use inside or out.

Some ideas for themes and content:

- Discovery: torch, paper, pencils, binoculars, magnifying glass, parchment with Hebrew letters, map of Israel.

- Home building: *mezuzot*, candlesticks, *Kiddush* cup, *challah* cloth, *chanukiah*.

- Biblical play: robes, head-dresses, jugs, toy camels and sheep, soft *Sefer Torah*.

EYFS Links

Principles into practice cards

In their play, children learn at their highest level.
L&D 4.1

Making dens and dressing up are an integral part of children's play and they don't require expensive resources.
L&D 4.1

Being creative involves the whole curriculum, not just the arts. It is not necessarily about making an end product, such as a picture, song or play.
L&D 4.3

Effective practice

Be aware of the link between imaginative play and children's ability to handle narrative.
(p. 116)

Planning and resourcing

Make use of outdoor areas to give opportunities for investigations of the natural world, for example, provide chimes, streamers, windmills to investigate the effects of wind.
(p. 79)

Activities for Immediate Impact
Provide a Simple Map of Israel for Activities and Games

Arise, walk about the land, through its length and breadth.
(*Bereishit* 13:17)

קוּם הִתְהַלֵּךְ בָּאָרֶץ לְאָרְכָּהּ וּלְרָחְבָּהּ.

Rationale

The Jewish people's love of Israel has lasted since God spoke these words to Abraham. However, introducing Israel to young children is challenging as it involves concepts of country, time and distance of which they have little experience. We have to bring Israel to them with images they can see, handle and talk about.

You will need

- A copy of the story 'A Visit To Israel' (see p. 80).
- A large weatherproof map of Israel or a chalked or permanently painted outline on the ground outside.
- Laminated photographs of places, buildings and people of Israel.
- Place names in Hebrew and English, for example, Haifa, Tel Aviv, Jerusalem, Eilat.
- Rubber rings, hoops, beanbags etc.
- Small-world resources, including Israeli flags and road signs.
- Picture cards of the sea, mountains and desert.

Getting started

- Read the story, outside if practical.

- Go out with a small group of children to find a good place to put the map or to find the one that's already there.

- Talk about the shape of the country, and the symbols for the sea, mountains, desert and towns.

- Challenge the children to find different ways to move, for example, crawl, hop or 'fly' from the mountains to the sea, or from the desert to the mountains.

Further ideas

- Play games using cardboard discs to represent Israeli 'towns', 'desert', 'mountains' and 'sea'. Provide beanbags/rubber rings for the games that follow:

    Can children throw a ring to try to land on a 'town' or in the 'desert'?

    With a child standing on each 'town', can they throw to each other and catch?

    Can they call out the name of the 'place' they are throwing to?

- Use the outline as a base for small-world play – add play people, cars, houses, trains, flags, camels, sheep, donkeys, palm trees and characters from stories.

- Provide 'walkie-talkies' for imaginative play.

- Provide programmable toys to give children experience of planning and controlling movements, for example from Haifa to Tel Aviv.

- Provide chalk for children to draw their own routes and create their own maps.

- Take 'luggage' and shopping bags outside for travel 'around Israel'.

- Play Israeli music outside.

- Play 'Follow my leader' – follow in the footsteps of Abraham, Isaac and Jacob.

- Provide photographs of places, buildings and people for children to examine (you could use old Israeli calendar pictures). Talk about these and place them on the map or on a nearby wall.

- Extend map-play to your own locality.

- Provide a range of maps for children to explore and use in their play.

- Go for a walk and take photographs which children can use to create their own picture map of the route.

Reflection

- Do the children use the map spontaneously for their own games?

- Are the children able to recognise the features of the map?

- Do adults create opportunities to talk about Israel?

Home links

- Look at road maps together.

- Show children a map of where they live, and other places they know well.

- If they have family and friends in Israel, talk about where they live and find the place on a map.

- Find Jerusalem on a map, atlas or computer.

Activites for Immediate Impact
Grow Sweet-Smelling Plants for *Havdalah*

> You are blessed Oh Lord our God, King of the Universe, who creates many sorts of spices.
> (*Siddur* blessings for various occasions)
>
> בָּרוּךְ אַתָּה ה' אֱלֹקֵינוּ מֶלֶךְ הָעוֹלָם, בּוֹרֵא מִינֵי בְשָׂמִים.

Rationale

There is a tradition that on *Shabbat* every Jew acquires an extra soul, a *neshama yetera*, that departs as *Shabbat* goes out and returns with *Shabbat* the next week. This is symbolised by the spices or herbs that are used at *Havdalah*.

For children to grow the scented herbs is a very powerful way of giving them ownership of the ceremony. They are natural gardeners, they are curious and they love digging. Watching a plant grow is a revelation for them. Through gardening with a Jewish purpose, not only do plants grow but children grow, too.

You will need

- Scented shrubs or plants, for example, lavender, rosemary, or scented geraniums.
- A magnifying glass.
- A 'growing corner' with the following:

  Large pots and compost for re-potting, or a garden plot.

  A large builder's tray to hold the compost.

  Watering cans.

  Trowels.

Getting started

- Set up a 'talk table' with a selection of scented plants that you intend to re-pot or plant out. Add magnifying glasses for close examination.
- Encourage the children to investigate and talk about what they see, feel and smell.
- Use leaves from the same plants for *Havdalah* and encourage the children to smell them after reciting the 'blessing over fragrant plants'.
- Introduce the idea of planting a *Havdalah* garden.
- Support children in organising the 'growing corner'.
- Involve them in all the stages of planting and watering, including clearing up.

Further ideas

- Keep picture books of trees and plants out of doors.

- If possible, go with a few children to the garden centre to buy plants.

- Investigate some of the oriental spices that are often used for *Havdalah*. They don't grow in the UK but dried versions are easily available in shops, for example, cinnamon sticks, cloves, nutmeg, ginger.

- Fill a builder's tray with earth; supply watering cans, pots, trowels and seeds for free playtime. Use seeds, beans or dried peas and watch them sprout.

Reflection

- Are children involved in choosing the plants for *Havdalah*?

- Do they treat the plants with care?

- Do they notice growth in their plants over time?

Home links

- Children can be involved in many gardening activities indoors and out. Digging, sweeping leaves, planting seeds and 'pick your own' farm outings will all appeal to them.

- Indoor plantings can include beans, carrot or turnip tops, and mustard and cress. Out of doors, try radishes, carrots, potatoes, lettuce, tomatoes and strawberries.

- Search for unusual scented *Havdalah* plants in your own garden or when visiting a garden centre.

Introduction

> You shall count for yourselves seven complete weeks, from the day after the Sabbath, (that is) the day when you bring the (first) sheaf which is raised up aloft. You shall count fifty days, up to the day after the seventh Sabbath. (*Vayikra* 23:16–17)
>
> וּסְפַרְתֶּם לָכֶם מִמָּחֳרַת הַשַּׁבָּת מִיּוֹם הַבִיאֲכֶם אֶת-עֹמֶר הַתְּנוּפָה
> שֶׁבַע שַׁבָּתוֹת תְּמִימֹת תִּהְיֶינָה. עַד מִמָּחֳרַת הַשַּׁבָּת הַשְּׁבִיעִת תִּסְפְּרוּ
> חֲמִשִׁים יוֹם.

Maths is everywhere in Jewish life. The counting of the *Omer* quoted above, the timing of *Shabbat* and festivals, the sorting of *Chametz* from *Matzah* at *Pesach* and the building of a *succah* are just a few examples.

Children soon learn the pattern of the week and look forward to Friday, with its special atmosphere and *Shabbat* party. This is a time to celebrate and reflect. Set aside a '*Shabbat* space' where, with the help of a responsive adult, children can talk about what they have been doing, what came first and what happened next. This involves mathematical thinking and language: the moment is a Jewish one, even if the content is superheroes!

The festivals are a mathematical gift. There is the round *challah* representing the cycle of the year on *Rosh Hashanah*, the seven *ushpizin* (biblical visitors to welcome into the *succah*), the daily increasing candles at *Chanukah* and 'all the fours' at *Pesach* – the questions, the cups of wine and the sons. These are all easy for children to experience and understand. Other more complex ideas can be built on over time.

Make a festival frieze at children's eye level to provide a visual reminder. Make a chart to recall children's favourite festival foods and activities. The pictures will become a magnet for excited talk, especially if they feature children in the group.

What matters to children?

- Time to work things out for themselves.
- Real-life situations such as baking *challah* for *Shabbat*.
- Real objects to handle.

Adult role

- Provide Jewish items to count, sort and order.
- Use mathematical terms in everyday situations.
- Value the strategies children already use to solve problems.
- Encourage them to use their own symbols to record amounts and numerals.
- Add to your repertoire of counting songs and finger rhymes.

Reflection

- Are Jewish mathematical moments recognised and shared?
- Do you regularly allow time for children to work things out for themselves?
- Do you provide a broad range of mathematical opportunities?

EYFS Links

Principles into practice cards

Develop mathematical understanding through all children's early experiences including through stories, songs, games and imaginative play.
L&D 4.4 PSRN

Value children's own graphic and practical explorations of problem solving, reasoning and numeracy.
L&D 4.4 PSRN

Effective practice

Show interest in how children solve problems and value their different solutions. (p. 70)

Sequence events, for example photographs of children from birth. (p. 86)

Planning and resourcing

Provide collections of interesting things for children to sort, order, count and label in their play. (p. 67)

Plan time when children can discuss past events in their lives. (p. 87)

Jewish Values in Action
Jewish Time

> He made the moon to mark the seasons; the sun knows when to set.
> You bring on darkness and it is night.
> (*Tehillim* 104:19)
>
> עָשָׂה יָרֵחַ לְמוֹעֲדִים שֶׁמֶשׁ יָדַע מְבוֹאוֹ. תָּשֶׁת חֹשֶׁךְ וַיהִי לָיְלָה.

In a world without clocks, the days were structured by the sun, the months by the moon. In Jewish tradition, Sabbaths and festivals last from sunset to sunset, and the Jewish months follow the lunar cycle. This is the rhythm of Jewish life that shapes the children's year and gives them frequent and varied celebrations to anticipate and enjoy.

Teaching the essentials of a festival in the time available is a challenge. In the autumn the festivals occur when new children are settling in, at springtime *Purim's* Ahashverosh merges into *Pesach's* Pharaoh with hardly time to draw breath. It is tempting to try to 'do it all'. Instead, select activities which meet the interests of your current group. Young children learn by doing, so the festival activities need to be active. Simple stories and hands-on experiences will have a lasting impact, and can be built on in succeeding years.

The passage of time is difficult for young children, and 'yesterday' is an elastic concept expanding to include past events, fact and fictional. 'I went to Israel yesterday,' or 'Mummy had a baby yesterday' may reflect the child's perspective rather than reality. Dividing time into manageable segments helps children to order events, which is a key mathematical skill. 'Jewish time' does just that. *Tefillah* has its set time, *brachot* are said before eating, and *Shabbat* is the climax of every week. Make a visual time line of the day, using photographs of the children at *Tefillah*, eating fruit etc. (see p. 63).

Even a birthday, the high point of a child's year, has its Jewish time. Find out the Hebrew date and have a second celebration (see p. 66)!

EYFS Links

Principles into practice cards

Schedules and routines should flow with children's needs. All planning starts with observing children in order to understand and consider their present interests, development and learning.
EE 3.1

Time is about how children find out about past and present events relevant to their own lives or those of their families.
L&D 4.4 K&U

Use mathematical terms during play and daily routines.
L&D 4.4 PSRN

Effective practice

Use and encourage children to use the language of time in conversations, for example, 'past' 'now' and 'then'.
(p. 85)

Planning and resourcing

Set up displays that remind children of what they have experienced, using objects, artefacts, photographs and books.
(p. 50)

Jewish Values in Action
Charity – צְדָקָה *Tzedakah*

Justice, justice you shall pursue.
(*Devarim* 16:20)

צֶדֶק צֶדֶק תִּרְדֹּף.

The word צְדָקָה (*tzedakah*) is usually translated as 'charity', but the underlying idea is justice for all. Sharing God's blessings with others is true *tzedakah* and can include giving money, clothing, food and time. Many settings use a *tzedakah* box at their *Shabbat* party, reflecting the Jewish custom of giving just before *Shabbat*.

The *tzedakah* box is a box of mathematical opportunities. Empty it with the children so that they can sort coins according to size, shape and colour. Encourage them to have a go at counting and recording what they find. Provide a variety of resources for sorting and counting, such as shallow trays, purses and wallets, number lines for matching and paper and markers for children's spontaneous tallies. Children's actions and comments will tell you a great deal about their mathematical understanding. See if they can find and recognise the numbers on the coins and if they know the difference between numbers and letters.

Link *tzedakah* to the cycle of the Jewish year and draw out the mathematical learning. Collect food before *Pesach* which children can help to sort, or fill shoeboxes with toys at *Chanukah* and work out how to fit them in. Collect outgrown clothing if the focus is 'Joseph's coat of many colours', or contribute towards baby equipment if it is 'Moses in the bulrushes'. Young children love the idea of being 'bigger', with its opportunities for ordering and comparing.

- Put play money and a *tzedakah* box in the home corner.
- Set up a charity shop for role-play.
- Visit elderly people to share a singsong.
- Make a book of *tzedakah* activities. Include the children's spontaneous drawings and mark-making showing different amounts.

EYFS Links

Principles into practice cards

Even the most ordinary events can be made more exciting and interesting when you give some thought to it.
EE 3.2

Plan activities that promote emotional, moral, spiritual and social development together with intellectual development.
L&D 4.4 PSE

Effective practice

Sort coins on play trays into interesting arrangements and shapes; sort them into bags, purses and containers.
(p. 73)

Planning and resourcing

Create opportunities for children to experiment with a number of objects, the written numeral and the written number.
(p. 68)

Encourage children to record what they have done, for example by drawing or tallying.
(p. 70)

Experience Israel Through Maths

And You, O Lord, are a shield about me, my glory, He who holds my head high.
(*Tehillim* 3:4)

וְאַתָּה ה' מָגֵן בַּעֲדִי כְּבוֹדִי וּמֵרִים רֹאשִׁי.

The *Magen David* 'The Shield of David', is one of the most important and familiar symbols of Israel. It is the main feature of the Israeli flag and children quickly learn to recognise it. It is associated with God's protection of Israel.

Look closely at an Israeli flag and find the different shapes. How many triangles can the children see? Provide some triangles and blue ribbons for children to play with. Some will make patterns and some may work out how to make a *Magen David*.

You could follow this by providing collage materials and/or paint to make Israeli flags; the process is more important than the result. Notice how children use the space on a page, and how aware they are of the different shapes.

Ideas to explore

- Add Israeli flags to the construction area, and attach small ones to bikes and trikes.

- Introduce the terms 'triangle', parallel' and 'rectangle'.

- Plant a *Magen David*-shaped flower bed.

- Make a birthday card for Israel:

    Give children a selection of card for their own design.

    Supply paper and tape for homemade envelopes.

    Encourage children to work out what size and shape they need.

- Make *falafel* and pitta:

    Can children cut the pitta in half?

    How many *falafel* can they fit in one pitta?

    Talk about size and shape.

- Teach children simple Israeli dances. Dance in pairs or circles, count the steps and clap 1, 2, 3 rhythms.

- Count in Hebrew (see glossary, p. 84).

EYFS Links

Principles into practice cards

Provide a range of activities, some of which focus on mathematical learning and some which enable mathematical learning to be drawn out, for example exploring shape, size and pattern.
L&D 4.4 PSRN

Effective practice

Encourage children to talk about the shapes they see and use and how they are arranged.
(p. 73)

Planning and resourcing

Plan opportunities for children to describe and compare shapes, measures and distance.
(p. 74)

Provide examples of the same shape in different sizes.
(p. 74)

Show pictures that have symmetry or pattern and talk to children about them.
(p. 74)

Number Ideas for
Jewish Seasons and Celebrations

EYFS Links

Principles into practice cards

Babies' and children's mathematical development occurs as they seek patterns, make connections and recognise relationships through finding out about and working with numbers and counting, with sorting and matching and with shape, space and measures.
L&D 4.4 PSRN

Effective practice

Motivate children to be active through games such as follow my leader.
(p. 96)

Involve young children in the preparation of food.
(p. 100)

Teach children how to use tools and materials effectively and safely.
(p. 105)

Introduce children to language to describe sounds and rhythm, for example loud and soft, fast and slow.
(p. 113)

Rosh Hashanah

Listen to the notes of the *Shofar* – a small group activity.

- Have a special *shofar* blowing session for the children.
- Listen for a long note and a short one.
- Count different patterns of notes (the *shevarim* is a group of three notes).
- Can children recreate the pattern with shakers and other instruments?
- Clap or tap out the pattern of the syllables of children's names.

Succot

Musical *succah* chairs – small group game (see story 6, p. 75).

- Introduce children to the *Ushpizin*, the seven traditional *Succot* visitors.
- Start with seven chairs named and numbered for each visitor.
- Play as you would traditional musical chairs.
- Dance round to music and remove one chair after each go.
- Those who are 'out' count how many 'visitors' are left.
- Can children remember the names and recognise the numbers?

Chanukah

Chanukah woodwork – for two children at a time; supervise as necessary.

- Set up a *Chanukah* 'talk table' with different *Chanukiot* and notice children's use of mathematical language.
- Prepare a woodwork table nearby and protect the surface with a piece of softboard.
- Add balsa and/or softwood and a stock of nails and lightweight hammers.
- Challenge children to create their own *Chanukiot*.
- If children are new to woodwork, show them how to use a hammer and nails safely and give them time to practise.
- Make the activity available throughout *Chanukah* and encourage children to have a go at making a *chanukiah*.
- Use the opportunities for counting and talking about shape and size.

Tu Bishvat

Shivat haminim discovery – a small group activity.

- The seven biblical fruits of Israel are the date, fig, pomegranate, grape, olive, wheat and barley.
- Collect and put out the seven fruits. (Wheat and barley kernels can be bought at health food stores.)
- Provide magnifying glasses, knives and chopping boards. Supervise as necessary.
- Look at the fruits and discuss shape and size.
- Count the different types of fruit. Can children guess how many wheat or barley kernels there are?
- Cut and examine the fruits; look closely at the seeds.
- Use them in fruit salad and/or soup.

Purim

Hat tower – a small group activity.

- Collect as many hats as you can, plus at least one mirror.
- Encourage children to try them on and look in the mirror.
- Does a hat make them taller or shorter?
- How tall is each child with one hat on? Two hats? Record their height on a chart.
- Can they balance more than one hat on their head at a time? How far can they walk without the hats falling?
- Can they build a really tall hat tower?

Pesach

Mystery bag for *Pesach* – a talk table activity.

- You will need a large bag that can be closed and a children's *Haggadah*.
- Collect *Pesach* items for example, wine, cups, *matzah* box, cushion etc.
- Display items on the table for children to examine and talk about.

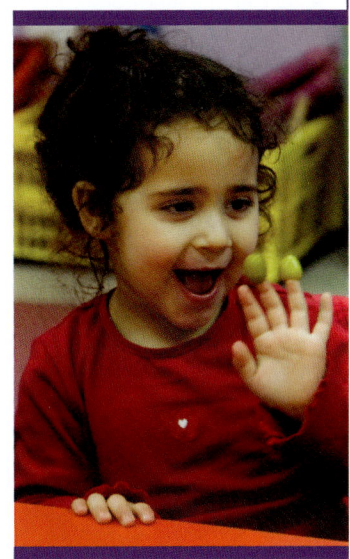

- Play games using the 'mystery bag':

     Put two items in the bag and ask children to work out what's missing from the table.

     Put all items in the bag, for children to take out and sort.

     Use the bag as a feely bag. Count how many items you have in the bag, on the table and altogether.

Shavuot

Milkshakes – a small group activity.

- Collect ingredients and flavours for milkshakes – strawberry, banana, chocolate, milk and soya milk.
- Collect calibrated jugs, spoons and whisks for stirring, mugs and straws.
- Children can pour their own milk, measuring how much goes into their mug, and count the spoonfuls of flavouring before stirring or whisking, saying the *brachah* and drinking.
- Encourage them to record their own milkshake recipe – notice spontaneous attempts to show quantity.

More Ideas to Explore

Shema

When reciting the first line of the *Shema*, the right hand covers the eyes to aid concentration. Learning to distinguish between left and right takes time and few children can do it before the age of six. As a first step, look at the symmetry of the body.

- Introduce clapping games, hopping on alternate feet, and practise putting on gloves and shoes.
- Provide mirrors for children to look at themselves and draw self-portraits.
- Make hand and foot prints and notice the position of the thumbs and big toes.
- Sing 'Put Your Right Hand In The Air' (to the tune of 'If You're Happy And You Know It') with a small group to help each child find their right hand before saying the *Shema*.

Bible stories

Immerse the children in biblical stories and give them opportunities to recreate them through:

- Mark-making and free drawing.
- Small-world play.
- Imaginative play and dressing up.

Listen to children thinking aloud as they play or draw. Often, the story emerges as the page gets covered in black because 'it's night time'. At moments like this, adults are privileged to see a flow of mathematical learning – language, memory and sequencing events – in a child's scribble.

Creation

Build up a number display or class book as you go.

- Day 1: Light and dark – provide dark glasses and torches for children to experiment. How can you find out what is in front of you in the dark?
- Day 2: Sky and earth – focus on 'above' and 'below' through movement and large-scale painting.
- Day 3: Grass and seeds – sort and compare seeds for size and shape, and measure growth from seed to plant.
- Day 4: Sun, moon and stars – draw around shadows at different times of day. What makes them change size and shape?
- Day 5: Birds and fish – examine a fish. A mackerel has lovely patterned markings. Can children make their own patterns? Cut open the fish and see what's inside.
- Day 6: Animals and people – play 'silly scoops'. Provide containers; children can collect animals and small-world figures from around the room to sort according to their own criteria.
- Day 7: Day of rest – create a *Shabbat* space where children can talk about their week and the things they have enjoyed.

Noah's ark

- Provide animals and different-sized 'arks'. How many animals fit in each 'ark'?

- Make a 'find the pair' game. Hide pairs of animals inside and out for children to find and bring into the ark.

- Provide a variety of deep and shallow containers, for example, builder's tray, baby bath, washing-up bowl, plus jugs and ladles for filling and emptying. Introduce words such as 'overflowing', 'deep', 'shallow' and 'flood'.

- Guess how many jugs you will need to fill the containers. How many were actually used?

- Go out in the rain, splash in puddles and watch them grow and shrink.

Eliezer's camels

- Collect a set of ten plastic camels and small-world figures for storytelling.

- Add them to the sand or create a small-world environment in a builder's tray.

- At snack time, provide jugs and beakers so that children can practise pouring out drinks.

Jacob's ladder

- Use a real ladder or an 'A' frame for children to climb up and down. Support less confident children. Count the steps.

- Create a ladders board game along the lines of snakes and ladders.

Manna

We don't know what *Manna* looked like, but it is described in the *Torah* as small and white, like coriander seed. Couscous looks similar.

- Provide a bowlful of couscous, with scoops, spoons and small bowls for scooping into portions.

- Provide a large bowl to represent the double portion on Shabbat.

- Talk about 'the same amount' and 'twice as much'.

Mathematical Moments

Principles into practice cards

Exploit the mathematical potential of the indoor environments, for example, enabling children to discover things about numbers, counting and calculating through practical situations.
L&D 4.4 PSRN

Effective practice

Introduce the vocabulary of spatial relationships, such as 'between', 'through' and 'above'.
(p. 96)

Planning and resourcing

Provide activities that involve turn taking and sharing.
(p. 33)

Counting and numbers

- One penny for *Tzedakah.*
- Two candlesticks.
- Three 'fathers': Abraham, Isaac and Jacob.
- Four species for *Succot.*
- Five books of the *Torah.*

Travel and distance

- Crossing the Red Sea.
- Wandering in the desert on the way to the Promised Land.
- A long plane journey to Israel.
- Round the corner to post *Rosh Hashanah* cards.
- Up and down Jacob's ladder.

Size and shape

- Square and round *matzot.*
- *Hamantaschen* triangles.
- Tall *Shabbat* candles, short *Chanukah* candles.
- Long thin *lulav,* small oval *etrog.*

Measuring and capacity

- Fill a water trough for Eliezer's camels.
- Watch the *challah* dough rise.
- Fill the cup to overflowing for *Havdalah.*
- How high is the *succah*?

Patterns and symmetry

- Stripes on a *tallit.*
- A border on a *kippa.*
- Stripes and *Magen David* on an Israeli flag.
- Curve of a rainbow.

Time

- The sequence of the nursery day – what happens after *Tefillah*?
- Yesterday we helped build the *succah*; today we are making decorations.
- How long until my Jewish birthday?
- A *brachah* before you eat, and 'thank you' afterwards.

Reasoning and problem solving

- How could we cross the Red Sea?
- How many pieces of *challah* do we need for our table?
- How can we keep Abraham's tent standing up?
- What shall we do if it rains when we're in the *succah*?

Comparing and calculating

- How many *Chanukah* candles will we need tomorrow?
- Let's share the apple and honey.
- How many foods in each *mishlo'ach manot* basket?
- Compare the different sizes of the animals in the ark.

Sorting and classifying

- Colour coding milk and meat dishes.
- Collections of *mezuzah* cases, *Kiddush* cups, Israeli and English coins, candles.
- Sorting the children's Hebrew and English names.
- Jewish objects for children to sort in their own way.

Visual Timeline

What happens every day at nursery?

Find your name

Tefillah

Free play

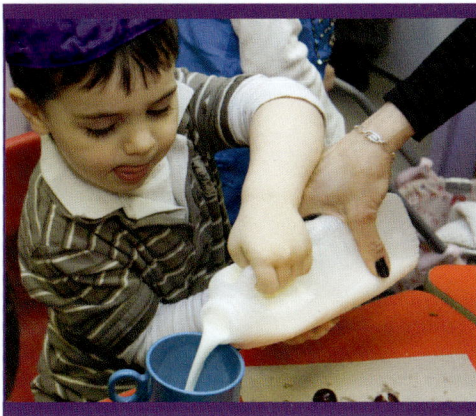

Snack time

Activities for Immediate Impact
'Jewish Number Lines'

Who knows one? I know one!
(*Haggadah*)

אֶחָד מִי יוֹדֵעַ? אֶחָד אֲנִי יוֹדֵעַ.

Principles into practice cards

Ensure that mathematical resources are readily available both indoors and out.
L&D 4.4 PSRN

Effective practice

Make sure children are secure about the order of numbers before asking what comes after or before each number. (p. 70)

Planning and resourcing

Make number lines available for reference and encourage children to use them in their own play. (p. 71)

Rationale

Children need years to develop basic mathematical understanding through everyday activities, handling real things. There are plenty of early years resources for children to count, but finding Jewish ones is more difficult. The first step is always to have real things to handle: candlesticks, *sevivonim*, *Kiddush* cups. When children have had plenty of practical experience, number lines are a way to give them counting, number recognition and sequencing practice.

You will need

To make the number line cards in advance:

- Pictures, photographs or computer images of Jewish symbols.
- A4 sized cards.
- Scissors, glue.
- Laminating equipment.

To play

- Sets of cards.
- 'Washing' line inside or out, with a bag of pegs.
- Space to move the cards around.

Getting started

- Make sets of cards you can change with the seasons. Use up to ten cards, but four may be enough for the youngest children.

  For *Pesach* you could have:

    1 baby Moses
    2 candles
    3 *matzot*
    4 sons
    5 cups of wine
    6 *seder* plates
    7 *Haggadot*
    8 eggs
    9 *afikoman* bags
    10 plagues

- Tell stories about the festival and familiarise the children with its symbols and customs.

- Include a set of cards on your festival talk table.

- Encourage children to examine them – notice the numbers and count the symbols. Can they find the items on the table?

- Challenge them to put the cards in an order that makes sense to them and peg them on the line.

Further ideas

- Children can take digital photographs of festival items and make their own cards.

- Use photographs of Jewish objects for number games for example, lotto, dominoes and memory games.

- Make Jewish number books.

- Count with a purpose at snack time. How many children want milk? How many want water?

- Encourage children to draw their own number lines and number pictures.

- Encourage them to use clothes pegs for other things, for example, hanging up dolls' clothes.

Reflection

- Do children count spontaneously?

- Are numbers displayed in all areas, inside and out?

- Do you highlight opportunities for counting in Bible stories or at festival times?

Home links

- Encourage parents to involve children in setting the table and shopping.

- Look out for numbers in the environment – buses, house numbers etc.

- Lend Jewish number books to families.

Activities for Immediate Impact
Celebrate Hebrew Birthdays

Pharaoh asked Jacob, 'How many are the years of your life?'
(*Bereishit* 47:8)

וַיֹּאמֶר פַּרְעֹה אֶל-יַעֲקֹב כַּמָּה יְמֵי שְׁנֵי חַיֶּיךָ?

Rationale

Every birthday is a reminder that life itself is a miracle. For young children birthdays are a source of delight and pride, markers in growing up. It is really important to be 'four', 'not three any more'. Most classes have a format for celebrating each child's English birthday; Hebrew birthdays can also have their own celebration. It may be impractical to celebrate individually, but *Rosh Chodesh* is the ideal time for a group party. Children will love the idea of a second birthday and it provides a child-friendly way of introducing *Rosh Chodesh*, the first day of each Hebrew month, and the Hebrew calendar.

You will need

- A Hebrew calendar covering recent years and the current year (use the Internet or Encyclopaedia Judaica).
- Children's English birth dates.
- CD of Hebrew birthday song '*Hayom Yom Huledet*' or similar.

Getting started

- Look up and record the Hebrew dates of birth of the children in your group.
- If you are planning to celebrate on *Rosh Chodesh*, note the English dates on which *Rosh Chodesh* falls.
- Plan a celebration on *Rosh Chodesh* for all the children whose Hebrew birthday falls in that Hebrew month.
- Invite parents to join the party.
- Celebrate! Use Israeli music and food where possible.

Nisan

1st Joey's birthday
7th Talia's birthday

Iyar

5th Israel's birthday
10th Rosie's birthday
12th Seth's birthday

Further ideas

- Make a visual reminder – a Hebrew birthday chart at children's eye level.

- Add a 'birthday cake' and candles to the Home Corner.

- Use the child's Hebrew name (see p 13) for their Hebrew birthday.

- Provide resources for making cards for the children's Hebrew birthdays. If possible, provide Israeli birthday cards featuring Hebrew writing and familiar characters such as Fireman Sam (Sami Hakabai) for inspiration.

- Include staff Hebrew birthdays.

Reflection

- Do children talk about their Hebrew birthdays?

- Do you name the Hebrew months when you introduce a festival?

- Do adults show interest in the Hebrew calendar?

Home links

- Send parents an invitation to the *Rosh Chodesh* party and include the date of their child's Hebrew birthday.

- Add the Hebrew date to your newsletters.

- When it gets dark early, suggest that parents and children look at the moon at different times of the month.

Sivan

6th David's birthday

Tammuz

21st Zak's birthday
25th Sophie's birthday

Introduction

And you shall tell your child on that day…
(*Shemot* 13:8)

וְהִגַּדְתָּ לְבִנְךָ בַּיּוֹם הַהוּא לֵאמֹר.

Storytelling has always been an essential part of Jewish life. Catching the imagination of a child with a compelling story is more than a pastime, it is a way of transmitting ideas, information and memories, family histories, lifestyles and values. The commandment to 'tell your child' the story of the Exodus from Egypt does all this and links the past to the Jewish future.

How the story is told holds the key to the child's enjoyment. The enchantment of a well-told story strengthens the relationship between teller and listeners and lingers in the memory. Words and pictures in the mind enable children to make stories their own and to share them with others.

The stories in this chapter are designed as an addition to your repertoire. Some are original and some are based on biblical or traditional tales. They are starting points to introduce activities in this book. Adapt them to suit your children and your setting. Have fun with puppets and props and engage the children in active participation.

What matters to children?

- Feeling that the story is told especially for them.
- Being able to hear or follow the story.
- Being comfortable.
- Having a good view of any pictures or props that are used.

Adult role

- Choose stories to suit the ages and abilities of your children.
- Keep up-to-date with new Jewish publications for children.
- Be flexible – tell stories at any time of day, to groups small and large.
- Listen to children's stories. Ask, 'What happens next?'

Reflection

- Are Jewish and biblical stories a regular part of your repertoire?
- Do all staff have the chance to tell stories?
- Do you adapt stories according to the children's reactions?
- Do some stories emerge in children's play?

EYFS Links

Principles into practice cards

Babies and children develop their competence in communicating through having frequent enjoyable interactions with other people in contexts they understand.
UC 1.1

Look at children's involvement in their learning as well as at the nature and quality of adult interactions in children's learning.
L&D 4.2

Warm trusting relationships with knowledgeable adults support children's learning more effectively than any amount of resources.
PR 2.3

Effective practice

Encourage children to predict possible endings to stories and events.
(p. 45)

Read stories that children already know, pausing at intervals to encourage them to 'read' the next word.
(p. 54)

Planning and resourcing

Introduce alongside books, story props, such as pictures, puppets and objects to encourage children to retell stories and to think about how the characters feel.
(p. 44)

Storytelling

Storytelling is a dialogue. When people exchange experiences of a party or an eventful journey, a story develops. Telling a story to children is an extension of the art of everyday conversation. Children want to help the story along and their interruptions can become part of the narrative.

The Bible is the traditional source of the most powerful Jewish stories. It is important to read the original and adapt it before sharing a story with children. Some phrases such as 'Where you go I will go' are embedded deep in Jewish experience and lend themselves to repetition, an essential feature of storytelling with young children. Others, such as the 'Binding of Isaac', are unsuitable. Care must be taken with any story to remain true to the biblical meaning and avoid misunderstandings. Children's comments, as well as follow-on activities, provide opportunities to gauge what they have understood.

The familiarity of biblical stories means they can often be told without a book. This gives the advantage of direct two-way communication with children. Facial expression, body language and tone of voice all bring the story to life.

Nowadays, biblical stories can be supplemented by a range of well-written and illustrated books on Jewish topics for children of all ages. There are suggestions throughout this book and new titles are appearing all the time. For up-to-date information use an Internet search engine.

- Know your stories; in particular, plan how you will start and finish.

- Be responsive and maintain eye contact with all children.

- Use different voices for different characters.

- Vary your facial expressions.

- Tell the story with gestures and movement.

- Use key phrases and repetition to encourage children to join in.

- Focus on a central character.

- Limit the number of people or events.

- Tell a long, complex story such as the *Purim* story in stages – build up the suspense!

- Introduce 'homemade' action songs and rhymes to emphasise key points in the story.

Telling a story with props

Story props can be:

- Soft toys and puppets.

- Hats and costumes.

- Books, pictures and artefacts.

Props must be a support, not a distraction, and handling them successfully takes practice. Keep props hidden from view until they are needed, but make sure they are easily accessible. If a child 'helps' to discover one, it adds to the surprise and anticipation of the story. You can create an imaginary dialogue with a puppet or soft toy and still maintain eye contact with your audience.

Alternatively, a hat or a series of hats is easy to use to signify different characters.

If you are using a book, use it as a prop – not as a lifeline! Try telling the story in your own words; ensure everyone can hear it and see each picture. Bear in mind that children may correct you if it is a familiar story! For experiential learning, collect items such as a *mezuzah*, hammer and nails to produce at the appropriate moment in a story.

EYFS Links

Principles into practice cards
Establish opportunities for play and learning that acknowledge children's particular religious beliefs and cultural backgrounds.
L&D 4.4 PSE

Effective practice
Be interested in children's responses, observing their actions and listening carefully.
(p. 107)

Sometimes speak quietly, slowly or gruffly for fun in pretend scenarios with children.
(p. 113)

Planning and resourcing
Provide storyboards and props which encourage children to talk about the sequence of events and characters in a story.
(p. 55)

Story 1
The Little *Shofar*

The little *shofar* rolled over in his warm soft cover. It seemed to him he had been asleep for a long time and now it was time to wake up. But everything was dark and quiet and he was alone.

If he thought hard he could remember a very different place, full of light and people. Then he had been singing so loud, calling at the top of his voice. All the people had been listening and then singing back to him in reply.

The little *shofar* tried to sing in the dark, but he just felt dust catching in his throat. No matter how hard he tried, he couldn't make a sound.

Then suddenly a little chink of light appeared, and he felt himself being lifted, still in his soft cover and placed on a table. A man with a kind voice said, 'It's just over a month to *Rosh Hashanah*, time to blow my special *shofar* again for the people in *shul*. I must practise and see if the *shofar* still makes the same beautiful sound as last year.'

The little *shofar* was so happy. He was going to sing again! He was taken out of the cover, lifted up, then felt a rush of air go right through him. He wanted to sing but what a strange sound came out. The man held the little *shofar* in his hands and said gently, 'Come on little *shofar*, you and I have to sing to God for all the people in *shul*. Let's try again together.' They practised and practised.

Sometimes the man and the little *shofar* made a squeak, sometimes a squawk! They tried to make beautiful sounds but it was very hard work.

'We'll do our best to sing beautifully won't we?' said the man to the little *shofar*.

'Our song will remind people of all the times they want to speak to God. Sometimes people are sad and they ask God to help them, and at other times they are happy and they want to say thank you to God.'

When *Rosh Hashanah* came, the man stood with the little *shofar* in the middle of the *shul*. The lights shone brightly and crowds of people stood waiting for the little *shofar* to sing. He tried with all his might to sing his very best sounds. The people waited… and then the man and the little *shofar* sang out '*Tekiah*'. It was loud and clear and could be heard for miles around. The man and the little *shofar* knew that everyone was listening to them. They were giving God's message to the people. 'Stay close to God and be kind to each other.'

Story 2
God's Musical Instrument

A long, long time ago, when God made the world, He saw the people and animals He loved and he wanted to gather them together to talk to them.

God wanted a special musical instrument that all the people could hear, so that they would come close and listen to what He wanted to say.

He called Adam, the first man, and said, 'Adam, please find a musical instrument that I can use to call all the people together.'

Adam thought, 'The harp makes a very beautiful sound.' He carefully made a frame and stretched strings across it. When he played it, it tinkled with a sweet sound. Adam showed it to God.

God said, 'The harp makes a beautiful sound but it is not very loud. Only a few people will hear it. I need something that will be heard by everyone.'

Adam was disappointed, but he went away and thought again. This time he made a shiny silver trumpet. It looked beautiful and it made a loud sound. He showed it to God.

God said, 'The trumpet makes a loud and clear sound, and it is beautiful to look at. But it is not a natural sound. Please find me a musical instrument that is made from a natural material and reminds everyone of the natural world I created.'

Adam was disappointed, but he went away and thought again. He looked around and saw rocks on the ground. He picked two of them up and banged them together. They made a loud noise. He showed them to God.

God said, 'The rocks are natural and they make a loud noise. But the sound is made by things hitting each other. I want my world to be peaceful and I don't want people to think about hitting each other. Please try again.'

Adam was very disappointed, but he went away and thought again. He found a ram's horn and he tried blowing through it. It made a strange sound – a bit like a cry, but very loud. He showed it to God.

God said, 'This instrument is natural, and it makes a loud sound. Everyone will hear it. It can make different sounds, it can shout and it can cry. This will be my special and wonderful musical instrument for calling all the people together.'

Adam was very happy and proud. At last he had succeeded. He used the ram's horn, the *shofar*, to call the people together. And it is God's special musical instrument that is used to call the Jewish people together for *Rosh Hashanah* and the end of *Yom Kippur*, so that we can listen to God's words and remember His creation of our beautiful world.

Adapted from a traditional story.

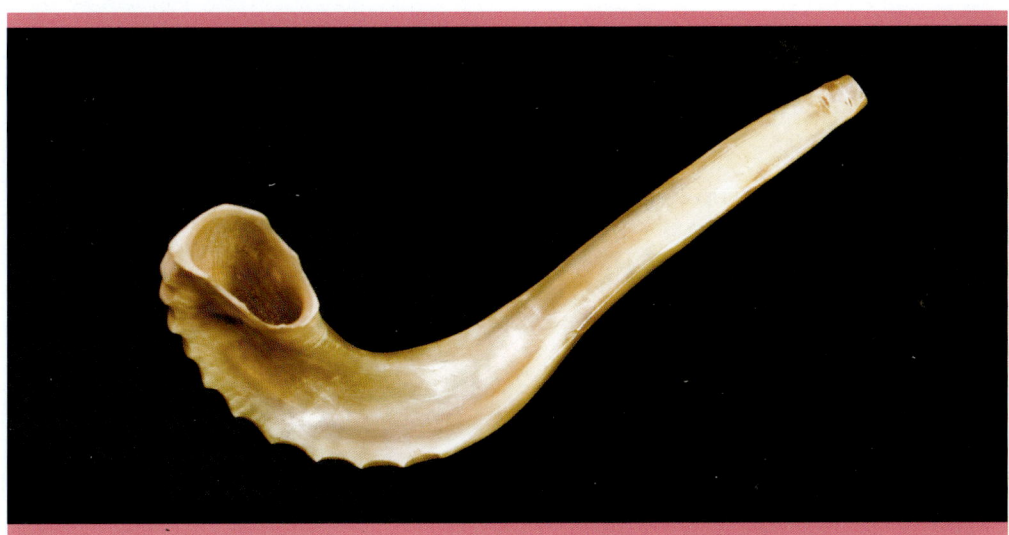

Story 3
The Story of Ruth

It was *Shavuot* afternoon and Liora and Zak cuddled up either side of Grandpa on the sofa. The big *Tanach* was open at a picture of two women walking together on a sandy path.

'Who are they?' asked Liora.

'Their names are Ruth and Naomi', replied Grandpa. 'They lived many years ago in *Eretz Yisrael*. They were both lonely because their husbands died. Naomi wanted to send Ruth back to her family but Ruth loved Naomi very much and didn't want to leave her. She said, "Where you go I will go," so they carried on together. They went to *Bet Lechem* where Naomi lived many years before.

'When they reached *Bet Lechem*, it was harvest time. The stalks of grain had turned from green to golden and everyone was in the fields picking the barley for food, and wheat to make bread. Naomi and Ruth were very poor and had nothing to eat. Ruth went into the fields too, and worked hard all day picking stalks of grain. This is called gleaning.'

'Cleaning?' asked Zak, puzzled. 'Why was she cleaning a field?'

'No,' laughed Grandpa. 'I said, gleaning. It means picking stalks of grain. In Bible times, poor people who didn't have their own fields were allowed to pick grain in someone else's field. That's gleaning.'

'Gleaning' chorused Liora and Zak. Grandpa smiled, 'Well done – a new word and an unusual one.'

He carried on with the story. 'The field Ruth worked in belonged to a man called Boaz, who was very kind to her. He told his workers to drop some grain stalks especially for her and told her to help herself to food and drink.'

'It's a bit like *Tzedakah*, isn't it?' asked Liora. 'Boaz had lots of fields and lots of grain and he let Ruth have some, by that gleaning word.'

Grandpa gave a big smile. 'You've got it, Liora!' He said, 'Well done.'

He carried on with the story.

'At the end of the day, Ruth brought a big pile of grain to Naomi who was very pleased to see so much. They could cook it and now they would not go hungry.

'Ruth told Naomi how kind Boaz had been to her. Naomi hoped that Boaz and Ruth would get married. She told Ruth to go to Boaz and ask for his help and that's what Ruth did.

'Boaz was happy to help Ruth. They did get married and before long they had a baby boy, called Oved. They were all very happy.

'Years later, Oved grew up and had children and grandchildren of his own. One of those grandchildren was David, who became the most loved king of Israel.'

'Wow!' said Zak 'We got David King of Israel, all because Boaz let Ruth glean in his field.'

'A little kindness goes a long way,' said Grandpa.

Story 4
Jonah the Prophet

Liora and Zak snuggled up on the sofa with Grandpa. It was nearly *Yom Kippur* and Zak had brought his special *machzor* to show Grandpa. He opened the page and they saw a picture of a little ship on a stormy sea. Zak said, 'Tell us this story Grandpa.'

Grandpa began, 'This is the story of Jonah which we read on *Yom Kippur*. Jonah lived in the land of Israel and his special job was to give people God's messages. One day, God told him to go to Nineveh, a big city, and tell the people who lived there that they were behaving badly. God was going to destroy the city and everyone in it.

'Jonah didn't want to go, so he decided to run away. He went to Jaffa and bought a ticket for the boat to a far-away town called Tarshish. They set sail, but soon a terrible storm blew up, with raging winds and enormous waves and the ship nearly broke in pieces. Everyone was frightened and they began to pray, except Jonah, who had fallen asleep. The ship's captain woke him up and begged him to pray for them all.

'The sailors wondered who had caused the storm. Jonah knew it was his fault because he had tried to run away from God. He said to them, "*Ivri Anochi* – I am a Jew and I tried to run away from God who made heaven and earth. The sea will calm down if you throw me into the water."

'The sailors were horrified at the thought of throwing Jonah into the sea because it was so stormy. They prayed and tried their hardest to row the ship to land but they couldn't. In the end, they did what Jonah told them and threw him into the cold water.

'Then God caused a miracle to happen. The sea became calm straight away, and God sent an enormous fish to swallow Jonah alive!

'The sailors on the ship thanked God for saving them, and Jonah thanked God for saving him inside the big fish. He was sorry he had tried to run away.

'Then another miracle happened, the big fish swam to the beach and opened its mouth and out stepped Jonah into the sunshine after three dark days inside the fish!

'God told him again to go to Nineveh and this time he did. He called out God's message loudly to the people, "In forty days Nineveh will be destroyed!"

'Every single person in Nineveh, even the king on his throne, cried to God for forgiveness and promised to tell the truth and be fair and kind to each other. God decided to save the city and all the people in it, after all. (End here for younger children.)

Optional extension

'Jonah was angry. He waited to see what would happen next. God prepared yet another miracle for Jonah – He made a large plant grow over Jonah's head to shield him from the sun, which made Jonah happy again.

Jonah the Prophet

Then God sent a worm to eat up the plant and it withered and died. The wind blew hard and the sun beat down on Jonah's head and made him faint and miserable.

"Did you really love the plant?" asked God. "I certainly did," said Jonah. "I can't bear to live without it."

'God replied, "You loved that plant, even though it only lasted a day, and you didn't work to make it grow. Nineveh is a great city full of people and animals. I created them, they are my work and I love them all. That's why I want to save them." '

Grandpa closed the book and looked at the children. 'What do you think God was trying to teach Jonah?' he asked.

'You can't run away from God,' said Liora. 'He's everywhere.'

'God helped Jonah lots of times,' said Zak. 'He saved him from the storm. He sent the big fish and it didn't eat him and He sent that plant to shade him from the sun. I think God loved Jonah very much, even though Jonah didn't always listen to Him.'

'I think those are lovely answers' said Grandpa, giving them both a hug.

Story 5
Honi Hamagal

The land of Israel is often very dry and very hot. Sometimes there isn't enough water and people long for the rain to fall so that they can water their crops and have enough for animals and people to drink.

Many years ago in the land of Israel, there was no rain, the water dried up and the people got very thirsty. At that time, a man called Honi Hamagal lived in Israel. God often answered Honi's prayers. People used to go to him and ask him to pray for rain. They said, 'Pray so that it rains.' He prayed, but nothing happened.

Then he drew a circle in the sand and stood in the middle of it and said to God, 'Master of the Universe, the people have come to me because you hear my prayers. Please send rain, I shall not step outside this circle until it rains.'

Immediately a few drops fell. He said, 'This is not the rain I asked for! Please send rain that will fill the wells, the lakes, the ponds and the rivers.'

Then rain began to fall in torrents. Honi said, 'I didn't ask for this either! Please send rain that is a blessing, neither too little nor too much.'

Just the right amount of rain began to fall. The thirsty people could give their animals water to drink and have enough to drink themselves. The rain would water the crops so that fruit and vegetables could grow and they would have enough to eat.

All the people were very glad God had heard Honi's prayers; so they went up to the Temple to give thanks to Him.

Story 6
Abraham's Visitors

Grandma opened the Big Book of *Torah* Stories and called Liora and Zak over to sit beside her. On the open page in front of them was a picture of four men sitting under a tree. The ground looked yellow and sandy, and there was a tent in the background. The men all had beards and Liora was sure they were very old. The sun was shining and the sky was a clear beautiful blue.

'Long, long ago,' began Grandma, 'in the days when the *Torah* was written, there lived an old man called Abraham and his wife Sarah. They lived in a land where the sun shone fiercely almost every day. The ground was sandy and the sand was very hot to walk on. In those days, people walked everywhere. There were no buses, no cars, no trains and no aeroplanes.'

'What about horses and donkeys?' asked Zak, 'and camels?'

'Yes, you're right' agreed Grandma, 'there were animals to ride on. But the people in our story were walking in the desert. A desert is hot and dry; there's very little water. So when Abraham' – Grandma pointed to the oldest looking man – 'saw three travellers, he was sure they were hot and tired and thirsty and hungry. He ran to meet them and he begged them to stop and rest under the tree.'

'That's what they're doing in the picture!' exclaimed Liora.

'The men came to Abraham, and he looked after them. He fetched water for them to wash their hot, tired, feet and gave them food and drink.'

'I've heard of washing hands, but washing feet's a bit strange,' said Zak. 'I wonder whether the water was warm or cold.'

'The *Torah* doesn't say,' laughed Grandma. 'But it does tell us that the travellers were really God's special messengers to tell Abraham and Sarah they would have a baby. Abraham and Sarah were both very old and they had no children; they really longed for a baby to care for.'

'Were they older than you Grandma?'

'Yes, much older than me. God's messengers promised them they would have a baby boy, and that they should call him Isaac, which means laughter – because he would make them very happy. And that's what happened.

'Abraham, Sarah and Isaac who lived so long ago, were the first Jewish family; they were the ones who began the Jewish story. Today, we are their family, their descendants; we are part of the Jewish story, too.'

Story 7
Water in Israel

Zak and Liora were in Israel for their summer holiday. Even though the sun was shining brightly and it was very hot, Mum had told them to put on their wellies and turn on their torches.

'Where are we going?' asked Liora, looking out of the window of the bus.

'On an underground adventure!' said Dad. 'We're going back to the times of the Bible and the days of King Hezekiah to find out how water came into the city of Jerusalem.'

Mum explained that in those days no one had water coming in taps to their own homes. If you wanted water you had to take a big jug, called a pitcher, to a well or a stream, fill it with water and carry it home. People who lived in Jerusalem had to walk outside the city to get their water. It was a long way, tiring and dangerous.

King Hezekiah had a good idea. He asked workmen to make a tunnel from inside the city to a stream outside. Then the water flowed from the stream into the city and everyone could safely collect water to drink.

Liora and Zak were going to walk through that very tunnel, which had been dug so many years ago, in the Jerusalem hills. They went with a group of people and their mum and dad, scrambling down to an open door in the hillside.

Inside the tunnel it was dark and the ground was uneven and slippery because it was wet. The tunnel twisted and turned and they had to hold on to the walls to stop themselves falling over. The water began to get deeper and deeper and before long the water was up to their waists!

The tunnel wound on and on into the darkness and, just as they began to get scared and thought that they might have to start swimming, they saw daylight! They had reached the end of the tunnel.

They climbed out, back to the warm sunshine and laughed as they emptied their water-filled boots. Sitting in the sun their clothes soon got dry and they realised that they were thirsty, hungry and ready for lunch.

The next day, Mum was reading the newspaper and she said, 'Hey, listen to this. You can visit the Israel National Water Carrier, and go down into the pipes that take water all over Israel today. It takes the water all the way from Lake Kinneret down past Tel Aviv. It's a bigger, modern version of Hezekiah's tunnel – don't you think that's exciting?'

'Wow,' said Zak. 'Are the pipes as big as me?'

'Bigger,' said Mum.

'Can we drink the water?' asked Liora.

'No,' said Mum, 'it needs to be cleaned first.'

'That's silly,' said Liora between giggles, 'we don't clean water, it cleans us!'

'I never thought of that,' said Mum, smiling. 'Would you like to go inside the pipes and see for yourselves?'

Liora and Zak looked worried. Dad looked worried too. 'Yesterday we went along Hezekiah's tunnel,' he said. 'It was dark and wet and a little bit scary. I've had enough tunnels for this holiday.'

'OK,' said Mum, 'but let's remember our wellies for next time. Then we can have an even bigger underground adventure!'

Story 8
The Lost Candlesticks

Liora and her mum pulled the big cardboard box into the middle of the kitchen. It was dusty and old and full of broken toys. 'Time to sort this box out and throw away the things we don't need,' said Mum.

Liora felt a bit sad. She could see a doll with a dirty face and no hair that she hadn't played with for a long time. But she didn't want to throw it away! She picked up the doll and said, 'I'll wash her face and put her with the other dolls. I'm sure they'll be glad to see her.'

One by one the toys were taken out and sorted. Then, at the bottom of the box, there was a surprise. There were two packages wrapped in old newspaper. Dust and black newsprint dirtied their fingers as they unwrapped them. Liora and her mum took one each. 'Wow!' exclaimed Mum as she took off the last pieces of paper, 'I'm so, so happy! Liora, quick, open your package, I've found a candlestick. Have you got the other one?'

Liora pulled the paper off quickly and out came a matching candlestick. It was black and covered in wax. Liora couldn't understand why her mum was so excited.

'I can't believe we've found these candlesticks,' said Mum. 'I thought I lost them years ago. Your Grandma gave them to me when I left home to live by myself. I loved them very much and I used them every Friday, to light the *Shabbat* candles. When I moved house, I looked and looked, but I couldn't find them anywhere.

'Now we can clean them up and use them again.'

Liora washed her doll and helped her mum clean and polish the candlesticks until they shone. They were beautiful after all.

On Friday night, Liora and her mum lit the *Shabbat* candles in the old candlesticks.

'They're old, but we love them just the same, don't we?' she said, as she cuddled her beloved doll.

Story 9
Moving House: A *Mezuzah* Story

Liora and Zak were moving house. They loved their home, even though it was a bit small and crowded. Zak loved the apple tree in the garden. He used to climb it and reach out to the ends of the branches for big green apples that Mum made into the yummiest apple pie. Liora loved sitting on the swing, pushing herself high into the air, watching the sky and the garden quickly dip and rise around her.

But the new house was going to be fun. It had more space; they would have a bedroom each, and the garden was big. Zak thought it would be great for playing football and Liora was looking forward to riding her bike around it. They had found a secret place behind a bush that was just right for making a den.

The removal men came to put all their furniture, clothes and toys on a huge lorry. There was one very important job left – taking the *mezuzot* off the doorposts. Dad and Mum went round prizing them off with a screwdriver. Mum locked the door and they waved goodbye to their old house. Liora held the *mezuzot* in a bag on her lap all the way to their new house. She was longing to get there and fix a *mezuzah* but she had to wait. They had to check that the writing on the *mezuzot* was still clear.

The children went to Mr Sofer, the man who checked the *mezuzot*. They watched as he carefully opened one for them to see the tight little scroll. He showed the children the tiny writing, all done by hand. He looked at every word, and read them what it said. It was all in Hebrew.

'I've heard those words before!' exclaimed Zak. 'That's the *Shema*!'

'That's right,' smiled Mr Sofer. 'In the *Shema* it says we should keep God's words on our doorposts. It reminds us that He is looking after us.' Mr Sofer made sure all the *mezuzot* were perfect, and soon Liora and Zak were unpacking them in their new home.

They each had a turn at fixing a *mezuzah* on a doorpost. Liora felt very grown up, saying the *brachah* and balancing on a stool while she hammered the nail in. Mum helped her balance and Dad held the nail. He got a bit bruised when the hammer hit his finger instead of the nail, but soon each *mezuzah* was fixed. Liora put a plaster on Dad's finger to make him feel better and then they all enjoyed tea in their new garden.

Story 10
The Special *Succot* Visitors

Succot was just a few days away. Liora and Zak were very busy helping to decorate the *succah*.

They made posters that said 'Welcome' in English and '*Bruchim Haba'im*' in Hebrew. Liora made a paper chain and Zak drew pictures of the *ushpizin* to put up on the walls of the *succah*.

'Sh'pizin sounds like sneezing. Why are all those people sneezing in the *succah*?' asked Liora. 'Or are they freezing?'

Zak didn't reply for a minute. He wasn't quite sure himself. Then he said, 'Shall we ask Grandpa? He's sure to know.'

Grandpa sat himself down with a child on each side. 'The *ushpizin* are our special guests,' he said. 'We can't see them except in our thoughts. They are invisible, but the story goes that they come out of the *Tanach* to visit us in the *succah*.'

'Why are they called *Ushpizin*?' asked Zak.

'*Ushpizin* is an Aramaic word that means 'guests'. Jewish people used to speak the Aramaic language many, many years ago. Do you know who the *ushpizin* are, Zak?'

Zak had just drawn them, so he counted off on his fingers. 'Abraham, Isaac, Jacob, Joseph, Moses, Aaron… I think I've forgotten one.'

'Who was Israel's greatest king?' asked Grandpa.

'King David,' shouted Liora quickly.

'Well done both of you,' said Grandpa. 'So that makes seven *ushpizin* altogether. Every day of *Succot* they all come to visit, but each day a different one leads. On the first day, it's Abraham, on the second it's Isaac, and so on. We stand up and welcome them because it's a great honour to have these wonderful people in our *succah*.'

'But Grandpa, where do they sit? If we can't see them we might tread on them or sit on their chairs,' said Liora anxiously. 'How can you offer them a drink or some food if you don't know where they are?'

'We might not have enough chairs,' said Zak. 'There are seven of them and four of us and you and Grandma, that's loads already. And we are having lots of friends, too. There won't be enough room.'

'Luckily the *ushpizin* don't take up space or eat in the *succah*,' said Grandpa. 'They want us and our friends to be really happy, especially friends who don't have their own *succah*. Don't worry, we'll all squeeze in.

'Now you two go and ask your mum for a nice cup of tea for me, and a biscuit for you. Then we can bring out the table and as many chairs as you can find to make the *succah* ready for all our visitors.'

Liora and Zak were going to Israel for the very first time. They packed their bags. Liora took her Flora doll. Zak took his football card collection. 'Remember to take your sunhats,' said Mum.

They found their seats on the plane. Liora squeezed up so that Flora had some room, and Zak opened his collector's book. 'Remember to do up your seat belts,' said the flight attendant.

They arrived at Ben Gurion airport. Uncle Moshe met them and they bumped along in his big old car on the way to Jerusalem. Mum unfolded a map of Israel, Liora held Flora up to show her the view from the window, and Zak kept dropping his cards. 'Remember to sit still while I'm driving,' said Uncle Moshe.

He took them to the *Kotel*, the last remaining wall of the Temple where people pray and put their messages to God in the cracks of the wall. Mum folded up the map, Liora showed Flora the enormous high wall, and Zak took out the card with his favourite player on it. 'Remember to put your own message in the wall,' said Dad as he gave them each a piece of paper and a pen to write their messages.

Uncle Moshe took them down to the Dead Sea, for a swim. The sand was so hot they had to wear shoes to walk to the water. Mum got the map wet, Liora took Flora into the water, and Zak put his football cards in his trouser pocket. 'Remember to pick up all your clothes afterwards,' said Dad.

In Eilat they had a boat trip in a glass-bottomed boat so they could see the multi-coloured fish and the pink coral. Mum found Eilat on the map, Liora shared her ice cream with Flora, and Zak licked his cards instead of the ice cream, by mistake. 'Remember to sit still in the middle of the boat,' said Dad.

They played on the beach in Tel Aviv. Mum got sand on the map, Liora built a sandcastle for Flora, and Zak flicked his cards as far as he could. 'Remember to wear sunblock,' said Dad.

They went up the Carmelite underground railway in Haifa. Mum showed them all the stations on the map, Liora dropped Flora under the seat, and Zak's cards fell out of his pocket. 'Remember to take care of your things,' said Mum and Dad together, as Dad picked up Flora and Mum helped Zak find all his cards.

They went to a restaurant with a lovely view over Haifa Bay. Mum got ketchup on the map, Liora helped Flora choose pizza for lunch, and Zak stacked his cards up on the table like a castle. 'Remember to leave some space for the food,' said Dad.

'So what do you remember about Israel?' asked Dad once they were back home.

'Flora got dirty but I can give her a wash,' said Liora.

'And I didn't lose any of my cards,' said Zak.

'Is that what you liked the best?' asked Mum.

'Well,' said Liora, 'We packed our sunhats and did up our seatbelts. We sat still in Uncle Moshe's car and put messages in the cracks in the *Kotel*. We swam in the Dead Sea and saw the fish under the boat in Eilat. Then we played on the beach in Tel Aviv and went up the railway in Haifa and Mum didn't lose the map.'

'And the best of all?'

'I was so excited when Flora really swam in the Dead Sea,' said Liora.

Zak said, 'It felt very special when I put my favourite card in the *Kotel*. My team's the best and I hope God looks after them.'

'Yes,' said Mum softly, 'We hope God looks after all of us, too.'

Story 12
Going up to Jerusalem

Liora and Zak sat in the aeroplane craning their necks to see through the window. They had waited so long for this moment. Beneath them they could see the seashore of Israel. The sky was blue and the sea sparkled.

Suddenly, they had arrived. Only minutes to go and they would be with their cousins from Jerusalem for the whole summer! They queued impatiently to show their passports and collect their luggage. Then the automatic doors opened and they walked out to a crowd of people. They searched the faces; their cousins, Yitzi, Avrom and Shoshi were running towards them, laughing and shouting, 'B'ruchim Haba'im – welcome to Israel!'

They all hugged each other, then they piled into uncle Moshe's 'taxi' – a big van, with torn seats and flapping sunshades. Hot dusty air blew through the windows. Uncle Moshe drove carefully onto the motorway; Liora held her breath with excitement as they turned onto the Jerusalem road. The brown fields became rocky hills as the road climbed and then swooped down into a valley. Liora looked at Zak. He had fallen asleep! But she couldn't shut her eyes now – she was sure she would see Jerusalem at the top of the next mountain.

There it was! The road wound upwards and there was a big sign, 'Welcome to Jerusalem', 'b'ruchim haba'im lirushalayim'. Liora could read the big Hebrew letters for herself. She saw an enormous bridge that was like a harp and they drove past big buildings and a park and into the parking lot by Uncle Moshe's flat. Hardly had they taken their bags out of the car when Uncle Moshe announced,

'First stop – the Kotel. Have a quick drink and let's go! That's the first thing you have to do in Jerusalem. You go and say a prayer at the most special *shul* in the world – the first ever *shul* and an open air one!'

'What's it like?' asked Zak.

'It's an enormous high wall, with a wide pavement called a plaza in front of it. It is the most precious place in the world for us because it is the only remaining wall of the beautiful Temple, the *Bet Mikdash* that once stood in Jerusalem. There is a story that this wall, the Western Wall, was built by the poorest Jewish people, and it was

especially precious to God who made sure it would never fall down. People sometimes write letters to God and push them in between the stones. You can do that too if you want to. If you've got a *Siddur*, take it with you.'

Uncle Moshe whisked them all away again in his old car, bumping through narrow cobbled streets. He parked and they all got out and followed him to the plaza.

Mum and Dad looked at each other; they had tears in their eyes. Mum squeezed Liora's hand and whispered, 'I'm so happy to be here.'

Liora was puzzled, 'Why are you crying if you're happy?'

'I'm remembering when I came here with my mother, your grandma, for the first time. I was the same age as you. One day, when you are grown up, maybe you will come with your own children.'

'Mum, write that down,' whispered Liora. 'That's my letter to God.'

Before they went to the 'ladies' section, they stopped to wash their hands. Liora walked right up to the wall, pulling Mum behind her. She found a crack and carefully pushed her letter in. Then they sang their favourite Hebrew prayers together. As they walked away Mum showed Liora how to walk backwards so she didn't turn her back on the holy wall of the Temple.

'Jewish people have been coming here to pray for two thousand years,' said Mum. 'It's the place we face when we are praying, wherever we are in the world. When we are in London, we look towards the *Kotel*, even though we can't see it.'

Mum took out her new digital camera. 'Please let me take a picture,' begged Liora. Mum agreed, and Liora felt very proud as she took her first ever photograph, a picture of her mum at the *Kotel*.

'We'll always remember today, won't we?' she said, as they gave each other a big hug.

The 'ch' in the transliteration of some Hebrew words is pronounced like the 'ch' in 'loch'.

abba
Hebrew term for 'Daddy'. At the Friday '*Kabbalat Shabbat*' ceremony, children take family roles, often at a central table. The '*Shabbat Abba*' recites the *Kiddush* and the blessing over bread.

Adar
Twelfth Hebrew month. A second *Adar*, called '*Adar Sheni*' is included in the calendar seven times every 19 years to keep the Hebrew, lunar calendar in line with the solar one.

afikoman
Portion of *matzah* that concludes the *Seder* service. Adults often hide it during the evening for children to find and claim an *afikoman* present.

Ahashverosh (sometimes spelled **Ahasuerus**)
The king who ruled Persia and made Esther his queen in the biblical book of Esther which is read on *Purim*.

Alef-Bet
Term for the Hebrew alphabet.

Amidah
Means, 'standing' and is the name of the central prayer of each synagogue service which is recited silently while standing. The *Amidah* is also known as '*Shemonah Esrei*', which means 18, the number of blessings in the original form of the prayer.

Av
The fifth Hebrew month.

Bal Tashchit
Means 'Do not destroy' and is the *Torah's* basis for care of the environment.

Bamidbar
Means 'In the wilderness', the Hebrew name of the fourth book of the *Torah*; in English, Numbers.

Baruch Haba
'Welcome' greeting to one person. See *B'ruchim Haba'im* below.

Bereishit
Means 'In the beginning', the Hebrew name of first book of the *Torah* – Genesis.

Bet Lechem
The Hebrew name for Bethlehem. The name means 'House of Bread'.

Bet Mikdash
Hebrew term for the Holy Temple that stood in Jerusalem in Bible times.

Bil'am
A pagan prophet who was asked by the Moabite king Balak to curse the Israelites in the wilderness, but blessed them instead.

boker tov
The Hebrew words which mean 'Good morning'.

brachah (singular) **brachot** (plural)
Means blessing. Blessings have a formal structure and are recited before fulfilling a '*mitzvah*', in appreciation of the wonders of Creation, and before eating and drinking.

B'ruchim Haba'im (plural)
Hebrew term of welcome, literally 'Blessed are those who come.' This was the greeting given by the High Priest to those who came to worship in the Temple.

challah (singular) challot (plural)
A *challah* is a braided loaf. Two are eaten on *Shabbat* to remind us of the double portion of *manna* that was given to the Children of Israel in the desert every sixth day, i.e. Friday, so that they had food for *Shabbat*. If they tried to save food for the next day on weekdays, it rotted overnight but the Friday portion stayed edible until the next day. Through this miracle, the Children of Israel learned how important *Shabbat* is in God's eyes, and how they should keep it.

chametz
Means 'leavened.' On Passover unleavened bread, i.e. *matzah* replaces regular, yeast risen bread. No 'leavened' food is eaten throughout the festival.

Chanukah
Means 'Dedication'. It is the winter festival which lasts for eight days (starting 25 Kislev) and commemorates the rededication of the Temple in Jerusalem by the Maccabees in 165 BCE after their successful rebellion against the Greeks.

chanukiah (singular) chanukiot (plural)
The nine branched candelabra used for lighting the *Chanukah* candles. There is one candle for each night of the festival plus the 'shamash' or 'guard' candle which is used to light the others instead of a match. One candle is lit on the first day, two on the second day and so on. The 'shamash' has its own position on the *Chanukiah* and remains alight with the other candles.

Chesed
A combination of kindness, love and compassion, usually translated as 'loving kindness'.

Cheshvan
The seventh Hebrew month.

Chumash
Chumash means 'five'. It is the name given to first five books of the Bible, also called the Five Books of Moses or the *Torah*, the holiest text and source of Law in Judaism.

chuppah
A wedding canopy.

Devarim
'Words', the Hebrew name for the fifth book of the *Torah*, which contains Moses' last words to the Children of Israel. Known in English as 'Deuteronomy'.

dreidel – sevivon (singular) sevivonim (plural) in Hebrew
A Yiddish word for the four-sided spinning top of a *Chanukah* game. Each side displays one letter of the phrase 'Nes Gadol Haya Sham' – 'A great miracle happened there.' Each letter has its own value according to the rules of the game.

Ellul
The fifth Hebrew month.

Eretz Yisrael
Hebrew term for the land of Israel.

etrog
A citron used as one of the 'arba minim', four species which are blessed and honoured on *Succot*. The others are the *lulav* (palm branch), the *hadasim* (myrtle) and the *aravot* (willow).

falafel
Spicy chick pea balls eaten in pitta bread. A typical 'street stand' snack in Israel.

haggadah (singular) *haggadot* (plural)
The book that is used at the *Pesach Seder*. It contains a traditional sequence of *Torah,* commentaries, stories and songs. See *Seder* for further explanation.

Hallel – A collection of psalms sung on festivals and *Rosh Chodesh* in synagogue and at the *Seder* service on *Pesach*.

hamantasch (singular) *hamantaschen* (plural)
Hamantasch means Haman's pocket. It is a three-cornered pastry, traditionally filled with poppy seeds, eaten on *Purim*.

Havdalah
A short prayer recited at the conclusion of *Shabbat*. A plaited candle, a glass of wine and spices are blessed, to mark the distinction between the Sabbath and the rest of the week. The prayer can be recited at any time from the conclusion of *Shabbat* until the following Tuesday.

Hayom Yom Huledet
Hebrew birthday song.

Hebrew numbers
1–10 in Hebrew – achat, shtayim, shalosh, arba, chameysh, sheysh, sheva, sh'moneh, teysha, esair.

imma
Hebrew term for 'Mummy'. At the Friday '*Kabbalat Shabbat*' ceremony, children take family roles, often at a central table. The '*Shabbat Imma*' recites the blessing over the candles and lights them.

Ivri Anochi
Means 'I am a Jew'. It was Jonah's response to the sailors when the ship he was in nearly sank in a storm (see story 4, p. 73).

Iyar
Second Hebrew month.

kavod
Term meaning 'respect' or 'honour'.

kashrut
Hebrew term for Jewish dietary laws. Food that conforms to these laws is 'kosher' i.e. permitted.

ketubah (singular) *ketubot* (plural)
Jewish marriage certificate. This document is sometimes beautifully decorated.

Kiddush
The prayer of sanctification said before *Shabbat* or festival meals. It is recited over a cup of wine in synagogue at the end of the evening service, often after the morning service, and at home.

kippa (singular) *kippot* (plural)
Hebrew word for the skull caps worn by orthodox men and boys. In some progressive communities women and girls may wear them too.

Kislev
The ninth Hebrew month.

Kodesh
Hebrew word meaning 'holy'.

Kotel
The Western Wall, the last remaining wall of the Second Temple.

Lag B'omer
The 33rd day of the 'Counting of the *Omer*'. The *Omer* was an offering of grain brought to the Temple for the 49 days between the second day of *Pesach* and *Shavuot*. The days of the *Omer* are still counted to mark the time between these two festivals. *Lag B'omer* is a day of rejoicing and weddings are often held on this day. The rest of the *Omer* period is overshadowed by memories of sad events that occurred at this time.

latke
The Yiddish name for the potato pancakes that are eaten on *Chanukah*.

lulav (singular) *lulavim* (plural)
The palm branch that is one of the '*arba minim*' blessed on *Succot*. See '*etrog*' for further information.

Machzor
Festival prayer book.

Magen David
Means 'Shield of David' and is the six-pointed star that is one of the symbols of Judaism and of Israel. A blue *Magen David* is the prominent symbol on the Israeli flag.

Mah Nishtanah
The phrase that begins the 'Four Questions' traditionally asked by the youngest person at the *Seder* on *Pesach*. It means 'Why is (this night) different?'

Manna
The food given by God to the Children of Israel to sustain them in their 40 years of wandering in the desert.

Masechet Barachot
A Tractate of the *Talmud*.

Mashiv haru'ach umorid hageshem
'Who causes the wind to blow and the rain to fall'. A prayer for winter rain in Israel that is added to the *Amidah* from the end of *Succot* until *Pesach*.

matzah (singular) *matzot* (plural)
Unleavened bread eaten on *Pesach*. This originated when the Children of Israel had to hurry as they left Egypt and did not have time for the bread dough to rise. It baked on their backs as they travelled.

Megillah (singular) *Megillot* (plural)
There are five books of the Bible referred to as *Megillot*, each one read on a different occasion: Ecclestiastes on *Succot*; Esther on *Purim*; The Song of Songs on *Pesach*; Ruth on *Shavuot*; and Lamentations on *Tisha B'av*. The term *Megillah* usually refers to the handwritten scroll of the book of Esther.

mezuzah (singular) *mezuzot* (plural)
A handwritten scroll usually inserted in a decorative case, placed on the upper right-hand side of the doorposts of Jewish homes. The scroll contains the first two paragraphs of the *Shema*.

Mishlei
Hebrew name of the Biblical book of Proverbs.

mishlo'ach manot
Means 'the sending of portions' and refers to gifts of food sent on *Purim* to friends and family. It is one of the four '*mitzvot*' of *Purim*.

mitzvah (singular) mitzvot (plural)
A good deed, one of God's commandments.

Mizrach
Means 'East', the direction of Jerusalem for Jews in the western Diaspora. It refers to a plaque placed on the eastern wall of a home or synagogue to indicate which direction to face when praying.

neshama yetera
Means 'additional soul' that traditionally attaches to every Jew during *Shabbat*.

netilalat yadayim
Means 'washing the hands'. This is a *mitzvah* accompanied by a blessing before eating bread. A two-handled cup is used.

Nisan
The first month of Hebrew calendar.

Omer
A measure of grain, particularly the barley and wheat offered to God between *Pesach* and *Shavuot*. See *Sefirat Ha'omer*.

Pesach
The Hebrew name for Passover, the festival that celebrates the exodus of the Children of Israel from Egypt. It is celebrated from 14–21 *Nisan*, in the spring.

Pirkei Avot
'Ethics of the Fathers'. A collection of sayings of the great rabbis and teachers of Mishnaic times, which is read a chapter at a time on *Shabbat* afternoons in the summer.

Purim
Means 'lots' and refers to the lots cast by Haman, the villain of the *Purim* story, when he selected a date on which the Jews were to be killed. The festival of *Purim* celebrates the saving of the Jewish people from Haman's decree. There is a party atmosphere in *shul* where the story of Esther is read. Children (and some adults!) dress up and everyone makes a loud noise when they hear Haman's name.

Rosh Chodesh
Means 'head of the month' and refers to the beginning of each Hebrew month which always coincides with the New Moon.

Rosh Hashanah
Means 'head of the year' and refers to the Jewish New Year which is celebrated in the autumn on the 1st and 2nd of the Hebrew month *Tishri*.

Seder
Means 'order' and refers to the family service held on the first night of *Pesach*. The *seder* follows the order of texts, interpretations, food and songs given in the *Haggadah* and the proceedings are initiated by the youngest child (or youngest person present) who asks the four questions, the '*Mah Nishtanah*'.

Sefer Torah (singular) Sifrei Torah (plural)
Means 'Book of the Law' and refers to the handwritten scrolls of the *Torah* that are kept in synagogues and read from on *Shabbat*, Mondays and Thursdays. The scrolls are treated with great respect. If one were to be dropped, the congregation would fast.

Sefirat Ha'omer

Means 'Counting of the *Omer*.' The *Omer* was an offering of grain brought to the Temple for the 49 days between the second day of *Pesach* and *Shavuot*. The days of the *Omer* are still counted to mark the time between these two festivals.

sevivon (singular) sevivonim (plural)

See *dreidel.*

Shabbat

Means 'Sabbath' and is a holy day of rest on the seventh day of the week, corresponding to Saturday. It lasts from sunset on Friday to sunset on Saturday, in common with the Jewish mode of reckoning, in which every day begins at sunset of the previous day, rather than midnight.

shalom

Means 'peace' and is a greeting used for 'hello' or 'goodbye'.

shalom bayit

Literally 'a peaceful home'.

Shavuot

The festival of 'Weeks', so called because it is held at the end of *Sefirat Ha'omer*, a period of 49 days (exactly seven weeks after the beginning of *Pesach)*. The Hebrew date is 6 *Sivan*; the festival is celebrated on the 6th & 7th in the Diaspora. It commemorates the giving of the Ten Commandments and is marked by the eating of dairy foods and a night of study.

Shema

The first word of the phrase '*Shema Yisrael*' meaning 'Listen Oh Israel' the foremost prayer in Judaism.

Shemini Atzeret

'Eighth day of festival'. It refers to the celebrations on the day after *Succot*. In Israel it combines with *Simchat Torah*; in the Diaspora there are two days of festivities.

Shemot

Hebrew name of second book of the *Torah*, Exodus. The Hebrew means 'Names' which is the second word of the book.

Shevarim

A triple note blown on the *shofar*.

Shevat

The eleventh Hebrew month, containing *Tu Bishvat*.

shivat haminim

Seven species of plants named in the *Torah* as native of Israel. They are: wheat, barley, grape, fig, pomegranate, olive and date.

shofar

Ram's horn blown daily in synagogue, during *Ellul*, the month prior to *Rosh Hashanah*, in preparation for the holy days, and during *Rosh Hashanah* itself. A single blast from the *shofar* marks the end of *Yom Kippur*.

shul

German and Yiddish word for school, refers to the synagogue.

Siddur (singular) Siddurim (plural)

Means 'order' and is the name given to the Jewish prayer book.

Sifrei Torah
See *Sefer Torah*.

Simchat Torah
The 'Rejoicing of the Law' celebrated with *Shemini Atzeret*. The Reading of the *Torah* is completed in one year and this festival marks the end of one reading and the beginning of the next. There are processions around the *shul* and a party atmosphere. A 'Bridegroom of the Law' and a 'Bridegroom of the Beginning' are honoured with the first and last readings.

Sivan
The third Hebrew month.

sofer
A person who writes Hebrew documents. The *Torah* and *mezuzot* are among Hebrew documents that are written very meticulously by hand, with prescribed tools and materials. The *sofer* is not only a trained professional but also someone who observes all the commandments.

succah (singular) **succot** (plural)
Means 'booth' or 'tabernacle' and is the name given to the temporary structures erected for the festival of *Succot*.

Succot
Festival of 'Booths' or 'Tabernacles' held from 15–21 *Tishri*, after *Rosh Hashanah* and *Yom Kippur*, in the autumn. It commemorates the time the Children of Israel spent in booths in the wilderness and also the harvest time in Israel.

tallit
Fringed prayer shawl.

Talmud
Volumes containing centuries of rabbinical discussions and learning, There are two *Talmuds*, the 'Yerushalmi' and 'Bavli', they were completed in approximately 500 CE.

Tammuz
Fourth Hebrew month.

17 Tammuz to 9 Av
The 'Three Weeks', a period of mourning for the destruction of the First Temple in Jerusalem. Nebuchadnezzar, king of Babylon, besieged Jerusalem for 18 months and broke through the walls of the city on 17 *Tammuz* 586 BCE. There were three weeks of fighting before the Babylonians reached and destroyed the Temple on 9 *Av*. Both of these dates are fast days and celebrations such as marriages are not held during the period.

Tanach
The Hebrew word for the Bible. It is an acronym of the first letters of *Torah*, Nevi'im (the books of the Prophets) and Ketuvim (Writings) which comprise the three sections of the Hebrew Bible.

tefillah
The Hebrew word for prayer.

Tehillim
The Hebrew name for the book of Psalms.

Tekiah
Single long note sounded on the *shofar*.

Teshuvah
Repentance. See *Yom Kippur*.

Tevet
The tenth Hebrew month.

Tisha B'av
Ninth day of *Av*.

Tishri
The seventh Hebrew month. *Rosh Hashanah*, *Yom Kippur* and *Succot* are celebrated in this month.

Torah
The first five books of the Bible, also known as the 'Five books of Moses' or *Chumash*.

Tu Bishvat
Means 'The New Year for Trees', held on the 15th of the Hebrew month of *Shevat*. 15 fruits are often eaten on the festival as a reminder of the calendar date.

Tza'ar ba'alei chaim
Care for living creatures. Jewish tradition places a high value on ensuring that animals do not suffer unnecessarily.

tzedakah
Means 'righteousness' and 'charity'. It is an obligation on every Jew, even those in receipt of charity themselves, to give to others. As implied by its twofold meaning the essence of *tzedakah* is integrity and consideration for others; it is not confined to giving money.

Ushpizin
The seven honoured 'guests' who traditionally visit a *succah*: Abraham, Isaac, Jacob, Joseph, Moses, Aaron and David. The word is Aramaic for 'guests'. These guests underline the importance of sharing the *succah* with the needy.

Vayikra
Hebrew name for the third book of the *Torah*. It means 'And He (God) called' which is the first word of the book. The English name is Leviticus.

Yom Ha'atzmaut
Israel's Independence Day, 5 *Iyar*. On that day in 1948, Israel's birth as a modern democratic Jewish state, was proclaimed by David Ben Gurion, later Israel's first Prime Minister.

Yom Kippur
The Day of Atonement, a day of fasting and prayer held on 10 *Tishri*. Adults spend the day fasting; synagogue prayers focus on *Teshuvah* – returning to God's ways and repenting for past misdeeds.

Yom Yerushalayim
This commemorates the day when Jerusalem was unified in 1967.

Brachot

This section contains all the *brachot* referred to in the book. It has been designed so that each *bracha* is easy to photocopy, for use indoors and outside.

Getting started

- Photocopy *brachot* you use regularly.
- Mount and decorate – a photograph of children carrying out the activity always works well.
- Laminate.

Further ideas

- Create a display that grows as you introduce new *brachot*.
- Make a class *brachot* book to keep in the book corner.
- Place *brachot* cards around the classroom for example, *brachot* for food in the home corner, the *bracha* for washing hands by the sink and/or water tray, and the *bracha* for seeing a rainbow in a weather box.

Blessings on the wonders of nature

Blessing to be recited on hearing thunder

בָּרוּךְ אַתָּה ה' אֱלֹקֵינוּ מֶלֶךְ הָעוֹלָם שֶׁכֹּחוֹ
וּגְבוּרָתוֹ מָלֵא הָעוֹלָם.

Baruch ata Adonai, Eloheinu Melech ha-olam shekocho ugevuratoh maleh olam.

You are blessed, Lord our God, King of the universe, whose strength and might fill the world.

Blessing to be recited on seeing lightning

בָּרוּךְ אַתָּה ה' אֱלֹקֵינוּ מֶלֶךְ הָעוֹלָם עוֹשֶׂה
מַעֲשֶׂה בְרֵאשִׁית.

Baruch ata Adonai, Eloheinu Melech ha-olam oseh ma-aseh vereyshit.

You are blessed, Lord our God, King of the universe, the Maker of the works of creation.

Blessing to be recited on seeing a rainbow

בָּרוּךְ אַתָּה ה' אֱלֹקֵינוּ מֶלֶךְ הָעוֹלָם זוֹכֵר הַבְּרִית
וְנֶאֱמָן בִּבְרִיתוֹ וְקַיָּם בְּמַאֲמָרוֹ.

Baruch ata Adonai, Eloheinu Melech ha-olam, zocheir
habrit vene-eman bivritoh vekayam bema-amaroh.

You are blessed, Lord our God, King of the universe,
Who remembers his promise, is faithful to His promise
and keeps His word.

Blessing to be recited on seeing trees in blossom for the first time in the year

בָּרוּךְ אַתָּה ה' אֱלֹקֵינוּ מֶלֶךְ הָעוֹלָם שֶׁלֹא חִסֵּר
בְּעוֹלָמוֹ דָּבָר, וּבָרָא בוֹ בְּרִיּוֹת טוֹבוֹת וְאִילָנוֹת
טוֹבִים, לְהַנּוֹת בָּהֶם בְּנֵי אָדָם.

Baruch ata Adonai, Eloheinu Melech ha-olam, sheloh
chiseir be-olamoh davar, uvarah voh beriyot tovot
ve-ilanot tovim, lehanot bahem benei adam.

You are blessed, Lord our God, King of the universe,
whose world lacks nothing and who created in
it beautiful creatures and trees for people to enjoy.

The English transliteration gives the *brachot* as they are said. The Hebrew versions do
not give God's name, as a mark of respect.

Blessings to welcome *Shabbat*

Blessing on lighting the *Shabbat* candles

בָּרוּךְ אַתָּה ה' אֱלֹקֵינוּ מֶלֶךְ הָעוֹלָם אֲשֶׁר קִדְּשָׁנוּ
בְּמִצְוֹתָיו וְצִוָּנוּ לְהַדְלִיק נֵר שֶׁל שַׁבָּת.

Baruch ata Adonai, Eloheinu Melech ha-olam
asher kidshanu bemitzvotav vetzivanu lehadlik neir
shel Shabbat.

You are blessed, Lord Our God, King of the universe,
who has sanctified us through His commandments
and commanded us to light the *Shabbat* light.

Blessing over wine

בָּרוּךְ אַתָּה ה' אֱלֹקֵינוּ מֶלֶךְ הָעוֹלָם בּוֹרֵא פְּרִי הַגָּפֶן.

Baruch ata Adonai, Eloheinu Melech ha-olam borei
p-ri hagafen.

You are blessed, Lord our God, King of the universe,
who creates the fruit of the vine.

Blessing on washing the hands before eating bread

בָּרוּךְ אַתָּה ה' אֱלֹקֵינוּ מֶלֶךְ הָעוֹלָם אֲשֶׁר קִדְּשָׁנוּ
עַל נְטִילַת יָדָיִם.

Baruch ata Adonai, Eloheinu melech ha-olam asher kidshanu bemitzvotav vetzivanu al netilat yadayim.

You are blessed, Lord Our God, King of the universe, who has sanctified us through His commandments and commanded us to wash our hands.

Blessing over bread

בָּרוּךְ אַתָּה ה' אֱלֹקֵינוּ מֶלֶךְ הָעוֹלָם הַמּוֹצִיא לֶחֶם
מִן הָאָרֶץ.

Baruch ata Adoni, Eloheinu melech ha-olam hamotzi lechem min ha-aretz.

You are blessed, Lord our God, King of the universe, who brings forth bread from the earth.

A selection of the blessings for *Havdalah*

The blessing over wine is the same as for *Shabbat*.

Blessing on smelling fragrant spices

בָּרוּךְ אַתָּה ה' אֱלֹקֵינוּ מֶלֶךְ הָעוֹלָם בּוֹרֵא
מִינֵי בְשָׂמִים.

Baruch ata Adonai, Eloheinu Melech ha-olam borei minei ve-samim.

You are blessed, Lord our God, King of the universe, who creates many kinds of spices.

Blessing over the *Havdalah* light

בָּרוּךְ אַתָּה ה' אֱלֹקֵינוּ מֶלֶךְ הָעוֹלָם בּוֹרֵא
מְאוֹרֵי הָאֵשׁ.

Baruch ata Adonai Eloheinu Melech haolam, borei me-orey ha-esh.

You are blessed, Lord our God, King of the universe, who creates the light of the fire.

Blessings to welcome festivals

Blessing on lighting the festival candles

בָּרוּךְ אַתָּה ה' אֱלֹקֵינוּ מֶלֶךְ הָעוֹלָם אֲשֶׁר קִדְּשָׁנוּ
בְּמִצְוֹתָיו וְצִוָּנוּ לְהַדְלִיק נֵר שֶׁל יוֹם טוֹב.

Baruch ata Adonai, Elohenu Melech ha-olam
asher kidshanu bemitzvotav vetzivanu lehadlik neir
shel yom tov.

You are blessed, Lord Our God, King of the universe,
who has sanctified us through His commandments
and commanded us to light the festival light.

Blessing to mark the beginning of a festival or celebration such as a bar mitzvah or wedding

בָּרוּךְ אַתָּה ה' אֱלֹקֵינוּ מֶלֶךְ הָעוֹלָם שֶׁהֶחֱיָנוּ וְקִיְּמָנוּ
וְהִגִּיעָנוּ לַזְּמַן הַזֶּה.

Baruch ata Adonai, Eloheinu Melech ha-olam
shehecheyanu, vekimanu, vehigiyanu lazman hazeh.

You are blessed, Lord our God, King of the universe,
who has kept us alive and sustained us and enabled us
to reach this occasion.

The blessings over wine, washing the hands and before eating bread are the same as for *Shabbat*.

Blessing on fixing a *mezuzah*

On fixing a *mezuzah*

בָּרוּךְ אַתָּה ה' אֱלֹקֵינוּ מֶלֶךְ הָעוֹלָם אֲשֶׁר קִדְּשָׁנוּ בְּמִצְוֹתָיו וְצִוָּנוּ לִקְבּוֹעַ מְזוּזָה.

Baruch ata Adonai, Eloheinu Melech ha-olam asher kidshanu bemitzvotav vetzivanu likboh-ah mezuzah.

You are blessed, Lord our God, King of the universe, who has commanded us to fix the *mezuzah*.

Blessings before eating various foods

Before eating biscuits, cake, crackers – any grain based food other than bread (made from wheat, rye, oats barley or spelt)

בָּרוּךְ אַתָּה ה' אֱלֹקֵינוּ מֶלֶךְ הָעוֹלָם בּוֹרֵא מִינֵי מְזוֹנוֹת.

Baruch ata Adonai, Eloheinu Melech ha-olam borei minei mezonot.

You are blessed, Lord our God, King of the universe, who creates many kinds of food.

Before eating fruit that grows on trees

בָּרוּךְ אַתָּה ה' אֱלֹקֵינוּ מֶלֶךְ הָעוֹלָם בּוֹרֵא פְּרִי הָעֵץ.

Baruch ata Adonai, Eloheinu Melech ha-olam borei
p-ri ha-eitz.

You are blessed, Lord our God, King of the universe,
who creates the fruit of the tree.

Before eating vegetables and fruit that grow in or on the ground

בָּרוּךְ אַתָּה ה' אֱלֹקֵינוּ מֶלֶךְ הָעוֹלָם בּוֹרֵא
פְּרִי הָאֲדָמָה.

Baruch ata Adonai, Eloheinu Melech ha-olam borei
p-ri ha-adamah.

You are blessed, Lord our God, king of the universe,
who creates the fruit of the ground.

Before eating meat, fish, eggs, dairy foods, sweets or chocolate or before a drink

בָּרוּךְ אַתָּה ה' אֱלֹקֵינוּ מֶלֶךְ הָעוֹלָם שֶׁהַכֹּל
נִהְיֶה בִּדְבָרוֹ.

Baruch ata Adonai, Eloheinu melech ha-olam shehakol
nihyeh bidvaroh.

You are blessed, Lord our God, King of the universe,
by whose word everything exists.

Shabbat

The Shabbat Box by Lesley Simpson
Kar Ben, 2001. ISBN: 1-58013-027-5.

Is It Shabbos Yet? by Ellen Emmerman
Hachai, 2001. ISBN: 1-92962-802-1.

It's Challah Time! by Latifa Berry Kropf & Tod Cohen
Kar Ben, 2002. ISBN: 1-58013-036-3.

Sammy Spider's First Shabbat by Sylvia A Rouss & Katherine Janus Kahn
Kar Ben, 1998. ISBN: 1-58013-006-6.

Where Shabbat Lives (Board Book) by Jan Godin Fabiyi & Sue Rama
Kar Ben, 1998. ISBN: 0-82258-946-4.

A Sense Of Shabbat by Faige Kobre
Torah Aura Productions, 1990. ISBN: 0-93387-344-5.

Shalom Shabbat (Board Book – Havdalah) by Susan Remick Topek
Kar Ben, 1998. ISBN: 1-58013-010-3.

My First Shabbat Board Book by DK Preschool
DK, 2003. ISBN: 0-78949-234-0.

The Littlest Candlesticks by Sylvia A Rouss & Holly Hannon
Simcha Media Group (NJ), 2002. ISBN: 1-93014-348-7.

Shabbat Shalom! by Michelle Shapiro Abraham & Ann D Kofsky
Urj Press, 2003. ISBN: 0-80740-873-5.

A Holiday For Noah by Susan Remick Topek & Sally Springer
Kar Ben, 1990. ISBN: 0-92937-108-5.

Rosh Hashana/Yom Kippur

The Hardest Word by Jaqueline Jules & Katherine Janus Kahn
Kar Ben, 2001. ISBN: 1-58013-028-8.

Sammy Spider's First Rosh Hashanah by Sylvia A Rouss
Kar Ben, 1997. ISBN: 0-92937-199-3.

Engineer Ari And The Rosh Hashanah Ride by Deborah Bodin Cohen
& Shahar Kober
Kar Ben, 2008. ISBN: 0-82258-648-7.

It's Shofar Time! by Latifa Berry Kropf & Tod Cohen
Kar Ben, 2006. ISBN: 1-58013-158-2.

Apples And Pomegranates: A Rosh Hashanah Seder by Rahel Musleah
& Judy Jarrett
Kar Ben, 2004. ISBN: 1-5801-323-0.

The Shofar Calls To Us (Board Book) by Katherine Janus Kahn
Kar Ben, 1995. ISBN: 0-92937-161-0.

Happy Birthday World. A Rosh Hashanah Celebration (Board Book)
by Latifa Berry Kropf & Lisa Carlson
Kar Ben, 2005. ISBN: 0-92937-132-0.

Succot

Hillel Builds A House by Shoshana Lepon & Marilynn Barr
Kar Ben, 1993. ISBN: 0-92937-142-9.

Sammy Spider's First Succot by Sylvia A Rouss & Katherine Janus Kahn
Kar Ben, 2004. ISBN: 1-58013-083-7.

Let's Build A Succah by Judyth Groner, Madeline Wikler & Katherine Janus Kahn
Kar Ben, 1995. ISBN: 0-93049-458-2.

It's Sukkah Time! by Latifa Berry Kropf & Tod Cohen
Kar Ben, 2003. ISBN: 1-58013-084-4.

Chanukah

Lots Of Latkes by Sandy Lanton & Vicki Jo Redenbaugh
Kar Ben, 2003. ISBN: 1-58013-091-2.

Harvest Of Light by Alison Ofanansky & Eliyahu Alpern
Kar Ben, 2008. ISBN: 0-82257-389-0.

Sammy Spider's First Hanukkah by Sylvia A Rouss & Katherine Janus Kahn
Kar Ben, 1995. ISBN: 0-92937-146-7.

Jodie's Hanukkah Dig by Anna Levine & Ksenia Topaz
Kar Ben, 2008. ISBN: 0-82257-402-6.

It's Hanukkah Time! by Latifa Berry Kropf & Tod Cohen
Kar Ben, 2004. ISBN: 1-58013-120-9.

Rainbow Candles. A Hanukkah Counting Book (Board Book) by Myra Shostak
& Sally Springer
Kar Ben, 2001. ISBN: 1-58013-031-8.

Hanukkah Oh Hanukkah by Miriam Sagasti
Kar Ben, 1995. ISBN: 0-92937-188-7.

Eight Candles To Light by Jonny Zucker & Jan Barger Cohen
Baron's Educational Series, 2001. ISBN: 0-76412-266-8.

My First Hanukkah Board Book by DK Preschool
DK, 2005. ISBN: 0-75661-105-7.

Tu Bishvat

Sammy Spider's First Tu B'Shevat by Sylvia A Rouss & Katherine Janus Kahn
Kar Ben, 2000. ISBN: 1-58013-065-3.

It's Tu B'Shevat (Board Book) by Edie Stoltz Zolkower & Richard Johnson
Kar Ben, 2005 .ISBN: 1-58013-127-8.

Grandpa and Me On Tu B'Shevat by Marji E Gold-Vukson & Leslie Evans
Kar Ben, 2004. ISBN: 1-58013-122-3.

Purim

Sammy Spider's First Purim by Sylvia A Rouss & Katherine Janus Kahn
Kar Ben, 2000. ISBN: 1-58013-062-2.

It's Purim Time by Latifa Berry Kropf & Tod Cohen
Kar Ben, 2004. ISBN: 1-58013-153-7.

The Purim Surprise by Lesley Simpson & Peter Church
Kar Ben, 2004. ISBN: 1-58013-013-4.

Pesach

Sammy Spiders's First Haggadah by Sylvia A Rouss & Katherine Janus Kahn
Kar Ben, 2007. ISBN: 1-58013-230-5.

Sammy Spider's First Passover by Sylvia A Rouss & Katherine Janus Kahn
Kar Ben, 1999. ISBN: 0-92937-182-5.

It's Seder Time! by Latifa Berry Kropf & Tod Cohen
Kar Ben, 2004. ISBN: 1-58013-092-9.

Let's Ask Four Questions (Board Book) by Judyth Groner, Madeline Wikler & Nicole in den Bosch
Kar Ben, 2001. ISBN: 1-58013-071-4.

Where Is The Afikomen? (Board Book) by Judyth Groner, Madeline Wikler & Roz Schanzer
Kar Ben, 1995. ISBN: 0-92937-106-1.

Only Nine Chairs by Deborah Uchill Miller & Karen Ostrove
Kar Ben, 1995. ISBN: 0-939049-413-1.

The Mouse In The Matzah Factory by Francine Medoff & Nicole In Den Bosch
Kar Ben, 2003. ISBN: 1-58013-048-6.

Four Special Questions by Jonny Zucker & Jan Barge Cohen
Francis Lincoln, 2003. ISBN: 0-71122-018-2.

A Taste For Noah by Susan Remick Topek & Sally Springer
Kar Ben, 1993. ISBN: 0-92937-139-9.

The Littlest Frog by Sylvia Rouss & Holly Hannon
Pitspopany Press, 2003. ISBN: 1-93014-312-8.

Shavuot

No Rules For Michael by Sylvia Rouss & Susan Simon
Kar Ben, 2004. ISBN: 1-58013-044-8.

Ten Good Rules by Susan Remick Topek & Tod Cohen
Kar Ben, 2007. ISBN: 1-580132-009-1.

Sammy Spider's First Shavuot by Sylvia A Rouss & Katherine Janus Kahn
Kar Ben, 2008. ISBN: 0-82257-224-4.

Israel and Yom Ha'atzmaut

Sammy Spider's First Trip To Israel by Sylvia A Rouss & Katherine Janus Kahn
Kar Ben, 2002. ISBN: 1-58013-035-6.

It's Israel's Birthday by Latifa Berry Kropf & Tod Cohen
Kar Ben, 2008. ISBN: 0-82257-668-6.

Let's Visit Israel (Board Book) by Judyth Groner & Cheryl Nathan
Kar Ben, 2004. ISBN: 1-58013-087-5.

My First Hebrew Word Book by Pepi Marzel
Kar Ben, 2005. ISBN: 1-58013-126-1.

Come Let Us Be Joyful by Fran Manushkin & Rosalind Charney Kaye
Urj Press, 2000. ISBN: 0-80740-731-8.

Joshua's Dream by Sheila F Segal & Joel Iskowitz
Urj Press, 1992. ISBN: 0-80740-476-8.

My Cousin Tamar Lives In Israel by Michelle Shapiro Abraham & Ann Koffsky
Urj Press, 2007. ISBN: 0-80740-989-3.

Israel by Marcia Gresko
Lerner Publications, 2008. ISBN: 0-82259-414-7.

Israel A-Z by Justine & Ron Fontes
Children's Press (CT), 2004. ISBN: 0-51626-811-8.

Lon Lon's Big Night by Miri Leshem Pelly
Milk And Honey Press, 2007. ISBN: 0-97906-562-0.

Jonathan And The Waves by Shira Sheri
Milk And Honey Press, 2007. ISBN: 0-979065-611-3.

A New Boy by Eve Tal & Ora Shwartz
Milk And Honey Press, 2007. ISBN: 0-97906-560-6.

Bible Stories

Sarah Laughs by Jaqueline Jules
Kar Ben, 2008. ISBN: 0-82259-934-0.

Abraham's Search For God by Jaqueline Jules
Kar Ben, 2007. ISBN: 1-58013-243-5.

Let My People Go by Tilda Balsley
Kar Ben, 2008. ISBN: 0-82257-241-1.

Bible Heroes I Can Be (Board Book) by Ann Eisenberg & Rosalyn Schanzer
Kar Ben, 2004. ISBN: 1-58013-124-7.

In the Beginning by Miriam Levin & Katherine Janus Kahn
Kar Ben, 1996. ISBN: 0-92937-195-5.

Noah And The Ziz by Jaqueline Jules & Katherine Janus Kahn
Kar Ben, 2005. ISBN: 0-58013-121-6.

Daniel And The Lions by Heather Amery
Usborne publishing Ltd, 2004. ISBN: 0-74605-436-X.

Joseph and his Amazing Coat by Heather Amery
Usborne publishing Ltd, 2003. ISBN: 0-74605-433-5.

Noah's Ark by Lucy Cousins
Walker Books Ltd, 2006. ISBN: 0-7445-992-5.

Jewish Life

My Jewish Home (Board Book) by Rabbi Andrew Goldstein & Kinny Kreiswirth
Kar Ben, 2001. ISBN: 1-58013-070-7.

A Mezuzah On The Door by Amy Meltzer & Janice Fried
Kar Ben, 2007. ISBN: 1-58013-251-0.

The First Gift by A S Gadot & Marie Lafrance
Kar Ben, 2006. ISBN: 1-58013-149-0.

Baby's Bris by Susan Wilkowski & Judith Freedman
Kar Ben, 1999. ISBN: 1-58013-053-0.

Good Morning, Boker Tov by Michelle Shapiro Abraham & Selina Alko
Urj Press, 2001. ISBN: 0-80740-783-7.

Good Night, Lila Tov by Michelle Shapiro Abraham & Selina Alko
Urj Press, 2001. ISBN: 0-80740-784-4.

Shavua Tov by Michelle Shapiro Abraham & Ann Koffsky
Urj Press, 2008. ISBN: 0-80741-084-4.

Goodnight Sh'ma (Board Book) by Jaqueline Jules & Melanie Hall
Kar Ben. ISBN: 0-82258-945-7.

The Bedtime Sh'ma by Sarah Gershman & Kristina Swarner
EKS Publishing, 2007. ISBN: 0-93914-454-9.

The Story Of A Torah Scroll by Eric Ray
Torah Aura Productions, 1998. ISBN: 0-93387-398-8.

Thank You God! A Jewish Child's Book Of Prayers by Judyth Groner
& Madeline Wikler
Kar Ben, 1993. ISBN: 0-92937-165-8.

Siddur Chick – Prayerbook For Young Children
Gefen Books, 2007. ISBN: 9-65229-382-4.

Va'ani Tefillah
(Hebrew only)
Korim Books, 2003. ISBN: 5-60001-555-9.

Siddur Shema Koleinu – The Interactive Siddur For Children
(Also available in an Ashkenazi version.)
Jewish Educational Press, 2007. ISBN: 9-65910-010-1

I Am A Torah by Beily Paluch
Hachai Publishing, 2004. ISBN: 1-92962-818-8.

Ten Tzedakah Pennies by Joni Klein Higger & Tova Leff
Hachai Publishing, 2005. ISBN: 1-92962-819-6.

EYFS

Practical EYFS Handbook by Penny Tassoni
Heinemann, 2008. ISBN: 4-3589-991-2.

Supporting Every Child's Learning by Vicky Hutchin
Hodder Education, 2008. ISBN: 3-4094-777-7.